UNSHAKABLE CONFIDENCE

UNSHAKABLE CONFIDENCE

A Practical Guide to Facing Fear,
Transforming Pressure into Power, and
Thriving Against All Odds

JOHN PIERCE

PEGASUS
Media World

Los Angeles • New York • Paris

Published by Pegasus Media World

PEGASUSMEDIAWORLD.COM

Library of Congress Cataloging-in-Publication Data

Names: Pierce, John, author.

Title: Unshakable Confidence: A Practical Guide to Facing Fear, Transforming Pressure into Power, and Thriving Against All Odds

Description: First edition. | Pegasus Media World, 2025.

Identifiers: LCCN in progress (print) | ISBN 9780978607883

Subjects: Career Management. | Success. | Business – Vocational guidance.

First printing October 2025

Visit JohnPierceAuthor.com and JohnPierceConsulting.com

To Mom and Dad

Amazing parents that I've learned to appreciate more
and more as I age and watch the sands of time pass

Each grain of sand a memory that makes friends and family smile

Is *all* that we see or seem
But a dream within a dream?

A Dream Within a Dream

Take this kiss upon the brow!
And, in parting from you now,
Thus much let me avow:
You are not wrong who deem
That my days have been a dream;
Yet if hope has flown away
In a night, or in a day,
In a vision, or in none,
Is it therefore the less gone?
All that we see or seem
Is but a dream within a dream.

I stand amid the roar
Of a surf-tormented shore,
And I hold within my hand
Grains of the golden sand—
How few! yet how they creep
Through my fingers to the deep,
While I weep—while I weep!
O God! can I not grasp
Them with a tighter clasp?
O God! can I not save
One from the pitiless wave?
Is *all* that we see or seem
But a dream within a dream?

—*Edgar Allan Poe*

CONTENTS

PART II: TRANSFORMING PRESSURE INTO POWER

PART III: THRIVING AGAINST THE ODDS

INFOGRAPHICS

From Dr. Nance Rosen
Author of the bestseller *Speak Up! & Succeed:
How to Get Everything You Want in Meetings,
Presentations, and Conversations*

WHY YOU MUST READ THIS BOOK NOW

When will you control your life and time? What have you been waiting for? Who did you think would send you a signal, tap you on the shoulder and say, "get in there," or lead the charge that took you up the hill? The truth is no one has—until now and this book by John Pierce.

It's not surprising that most people don't take control of their careers or lives, or even think about the time that's ticking by, because they are just waiting for something to happen. They are waiting for their lives to start—or start getting good, maybe even getting great ... someday.

After all, you've probably been seduced by the perfectly managed influencers, celebrities, or high- profile winners that you witness or hear about. The meticulously trained, groomed, and ready-to-go showoffs who are waited on, fretted over, and feted by millions of fans. The people who make getting out there and competing seem glamorous and fantastic. The gladiators in every sport or enterprise who are told exactly when to start their competitions or exhibitions, with rules that are clearly spelled out (if occasionally overlooked for the more famous among us).

Formula One drivers all complete a warm-up lap, then line up in their qualifying positions, and finally gun their engines as they wait for five red lights on the starting signal to go out simultaneously.

Marathon runners gather at the starting line. Elite runners typically enjoy a front row spot, with the remaining competitors starting behind them in waves. No one moves until a gunshot or horn signals the start of the race.

In the Kentucky Derby, horses and their riders are loaded into individual starting gates. A bell rings, and the gates spring open simultaneously, releasing the competitors onto the track.

NBA and WNBA games begin with a jump ball. NHL games begin with a face-off at center ice, when the referee drops a puck between two players.

Major league baseball games start with the home team in the outfield and the first pitch is thrown. The NFL and major league soccer games start with a coin toss, and the captain, who called whatever is face up, chooses to kick or receive the ball.

Makes you wish that competing in your career was so straight forward. Maybe you always thought it would be. A light would flash, a bell would ring, or someone one would toss a coin, and you would call heads or tails.

Maybe you are discouraged, angry, confused, anxious, or ready to throw your hands up in defeat because nothing about getting ahead—much less winning—seems clear to you.

Office politics, favoritism, intentional or accidental deception, and a complete lack of fairness or forgiveness can permeate your workplace. It's easy to believe that you can trade one bad boss for better one. One set of difficult clients for better ones. One dull group of co-workers for a livelier, friendlier bunch. One stuffy, uncaring corporation for an inclusive, compassionate company. If that's the dream and you're the dreamer, you haven't taken control of your career or life—yet.

Wishing won't make things right—you tried that.

Trading one company for another is rarely the oasis you were thirsty for. Until you take control of how you are living your corporate career, and what you are doing to control your own life and time, you are simply conjuring up a mirage.

The real magic, along with immense power and control, resides in you and your ability to see situations clearly, identify the people who can truly help you, and strengthen your inner resources including praising and developing your own talents.

You ARE at the starting line. And, you have the right guide to success in your hands (or if you're listening to the audiobook—in your ears).

You can't wait any longer to hear or see some external sign, like a horn or an attaboy or attagirl, to tell you that you are in this to win this.

You have every right to be the one who says, "it doesn't feel like work because I love what I do to make a living."

You simply must take control of your career, your life, and your time. You must make the rules you live by and succeed with. You must learn the actual seasons of your career and life, like patience, acceleration, coasting, grinding it out, and celebrating.

You must be the one to pioneer the path when no one has come before you or take the path of least resistance whenever you see one.

This book is all about all of that. About how you succeed in a world filled with obstacles, some that you must overpower and some that you can slide by.

In a unique combination of hard punching truths, enlightening analogies, sophisticated yet practical tips, reflections from personal connections, and a wealth of assessments that help you put your life into focus—this is the book that gets you up in the morning and marches with you all the way to the top of the mountain (or wherever you see success for yourself).

You will find everything you need to succeed between the work John Pierce has done for you in this book and the work he will guide you to do for yourself in the exercises and worksheets.

Do it all so you can have it all. Yes, it's called *Unshakable Confidence* for a reason. It's what you need and now you can have it. Read on!

Nance Rosen, MBA, EdD
Bel Air, California
July 2025

INTRODUCTION

To live a good life: We have the potential for it. If we learn to be indifferent to what makes no difference.

—Marcus Aurelius

All desire flows from grief. Anger, rage, jealousy, sadness, and a range of red-hot emotions that flare and fester can be violently painful (but very useful for a while) when the initial injury, insult, loss, or sucker-punch lands on you. Events like being fired. Passed over for a promotion. Witnessing the market crash when you just invested your savings and bought a house. Broken by a divorce or big break-up. Struck down by an incapacitating illness or an accident. Devastated by a dear one's death. Moved across the country, leaving everyone and everything familiar for a job or romance that doesn't work out.

Not one of us will be immune from any of this.

You may have heard that life isn't fair. You put in the effort. Do all the right things—or a bunch of them, anyway. Skimp or sacrifice to put acorns away in case a harsh winter comes—and then discover your acorn storage was blown to bits by a tornado.

It's not just that life isn't fair, sometimes it makes no sense whatsoever. You watch bad guys and bullies do great. The least talented and hardworking are crowned and celebrated. Cheaters prosper.

1

If you are not yet fully grown up by the time something awful happens to you, you will be after it does. If you haven't seen good things happen to bad people and bad things happen to good ones, buckle up.

In the aftermath—once the damage is cleared and you are left to soldier on—you may discover you're left with a gigantic hole in your self-confidence. That hole was filled for a while with the tidal wave of anger, rage, jealousy, and sadness that rushed in when you got fired, left, hurt, lost, or left.

When the big emotions recede, you are merely human. You are no longer the Incredible Hulk or if you made another choice, Ant-Man.

In so many ways, I wrote this book because I suffered a whopping loss and knew you would suffer one, too. In fact, because I am way grown up, I suffered a bunch of losses over a multi-decade career, and I know you will, too.

Because I am a man of Faith, as much as I am a Taekwondo blackbelt about to complete my 14th Ironman (largely because I need to add another stripe to the 13 already on my right calf), my desire to create a guidebook for unshakable confidence arose from what may be the last sucker punch of my corporate career.

When It Gets Real, It Hurts.

My goal is to help you not just recover from the inevitable injuries and losses you will face, but to train you to expect them so you will be ready, hardy, and resilient when they happen. Unshakable confidence boils down to compressing the time between injury and recovery—and accelerating your progress toward your goals, no matter what else happens around you (or to you). It's about not being surprised when you experience of collapse of normal because you know "normal" is a temporary condition—and all things, good and bad, pass.

I have been wildly successful in some of the meanest, cutthroat environments ever constructed by human beings (at least the corporate ones). These are organizations in a sector designed to have no mercy, leniency, or forgiveness, because they are run for one purpose: to make money according to rules that can change in an instant, with no warning. This would be the financial sector of the global economy.

Shareholders, regulations, change of ownership, new management, a shift in business models, the rise of competition, weather, technology, politics, fads, …

you name it, the firms in this sector might suddenly contract, convulse, or otherwise shake off or shake out people who are working in them. I've even survived a so-called mentor who, in fact, was a silent assassin of my career aspirations. Some events and bad actors are foreseeable. Others for sure will blindside you.

My experience in the financial sector, working with some of the most important players in it, has given me the financial security and lifestyle that have more than compensated me for the pain. But that's like saying that an MMA cage fighter is well-paid. He's also beat up.

The whole point of training hard before a fight—and having a strategy to win and live to fight another day—is why I wrote this book for you. You will get beat up. You will be in pain. You will be angry. You should not lose your confidence. You should live to fight another day. This book is all about what to expect, how to pick your fights, punch above your weight class, what to do when you've been knocked down—or out—and how to be a contender at every stage of your career.

Terrible? Wonderful!

Now, with all that brutal truth, I would be remiss if I did not flag how many wonderful, truly awesome, and inspiring people will be in your path if you make the journey. My best friends, people who have influenced my life and made me a better man, and those who unleashed my greatest talent are all from my career. Mentors who gave me their time and energy—taught me how to build relationships and orchestrate my trajectory—all came from the firms that employed me. Colleagues and competitors who shared their insights and rooted me on, all came from this industry. The people who today seek my advice and stay connected, real friends and the folks who matter to me, are from the decades I spent in business at different firms during some of the most challenging times as well as the gravy days.

In fact, other than my family, most of the people whom I have grown close to and shared history with, are those I met during my career or because of my career. So, take heart that what roughs you up also delivers some of the best friends and most rewarding times you will have.

Consider that most of your life is shaped by the decisions, responses, skills, and attitude you bring to events that are largely uncontrollable. That is why I want you to take responsibility for everything you *do* control. Throughout this book, you will feel my encouragement, okay pushiness, to save your money, create a network of trusted advisors and mentors, and be ready to move at a moment's notice. Take responsibility for educating yourself and building skills before you need them.

Learned and Earned Knowledge Both Count.

At various points in my career, I saw the value of returning to higher education. I earned my MBA at the University of London and then a doctorate in education at the University of Pennsylvania in the Chief Learning Officer program. Of the many reasons you want to refresh and enlarge your knowledge base, you may find that the cohort of like-minded professionals will be close to the top of benefits. Expand your circle with smart people who are in different sectors or professions. In this book, you will be meeting some of those from my academic life (as well as my professional one), as you read the reflections from my connections. And, while you can always watch a Ted Talk or listen to a podcast series on a topic to reinvigorate your perspective, there is something larger that happens when you commit to the academic rigor of a formal education.

In other words, arm yourself cognitively, financially, emotionally, spiritually, physically, and socially for what a successful career demands of you. The only way you can navigate the road ahead with confidence is to have strength in all these dimensions—because at various times, one will be more important than another.

Sometimes to face fear you might just need the physical strength to quite literally put one foot in front of the other (I know, I ran a 100-kilometer race just to see if I could). Other times, the investment you made in your spiritual life through a regular practice of your faith will be the miracle that transforms otherwise unbearable pressure into power. And it could be that the money you socked away during the good times is what allows you to thrive against all the odds when you see what's stacked against you. Why you prevail—and how you prevail—will be a function of whether you have built unshakable confidence in yourself.

The desire I have in writing this book comes from the grief I've confronted at every step of my career. Overcoming the worst has meant I could enjoy the very best of what a career delivers. The unshakable confidence I've earned is a gift, and I want to pass that on to you, as you make your way in the world.

John Pierce
Juno Beach, Florida
or Breckenridge, Colorado
(depending on the season)

P.S. You can continue to connect with me at JohnPierceConsulting.com— where you'll find more articles, audios, worksheets, and ways to work with me or invite me to come speak. You'll also find me on LinkedIn at www.linkedin. com/in/john-pierce-20ab946 and on other social media. Stay connected!

HOW TO USE THIS BOOK

You have a myriad of ways to benefit from this book and gain unshakable confidence, because you can use it in the way that works best for you. It's organized so you can progress from one stage to the next—with the book's subtitle providing the basis for the three central parts. After you make your way through this introduction and preparation, you begin your journey to unshakable confidence in earnest. Part One is Facing Fear. Part Two is Transforming Pressure into Power. Part Three is Thriving Against All Odds. Then, you'll find what I believe is a universal tonic for what ails us all in Part Four, Seeing the Light. Unless you have a burning issue that calls out to you in a specific part, I recommend you read the parts in regular order. Of course, you may also browse through the Contents pages and find specific chapters and other assets that feel like they are yelling, "read me first!" My best advice is you do you because you know you.

In each part, you get chapters with insights, stories, and analogies to enlighten you, plus practical tips to use immediately. At the end of each chapter, you're given an exercise, a question to reflect on, and a first step. In other words, this book is about making the transformations in your thoughts, feelings, and actions that catapult your genuine self-confidence to the next level (or quite a bit higher than that).

You'll also find the personal reflections of my extraordinary connections who share their own stories of obstacles and success, giving you an inside look into what achievement really takes—and how to bear up during the worst of times, make the climb toward the best of times, and celebrate your tenacity under all conditions. I've added in my own reflections to help you gain some perspective about what shaped my journey and why I can honestly say, "I've been there."

In addition, you'll find some infographics to help you distill some of the most important concepts in your confidence building journey and several quotations that I selected to keep you inspired.

Perhaps most uniquely in this book, you'll find in-depth assessments that may take you on deep journeys into self-acceptance and future-proofing yourself. These assessments help you build out assets that will support you in every aspect of your life as you progress (or stall) in your career, and develop greater savvy in the corporate environment. They will prompt you to personalize the learnings you get from reading. When you complete the assessments, you are in effect, a co-author of your very own version of this book—so it becomes your career book. You might do the assessments when they appear or you might set aside time when you work your way through them.

My goal has been to provide with you with a plethora of options that you can use as you see fit. I believe in you—your intelligence, your tenacity, and your trajectory.

PIERCE RULES
A Quick Primer of Life Principles

RULE 1: LIVE ON COURSE, NOT OF COURSE

Every day, you have a choice: to act with intention or to react out of habit. Choose to set a course for your life that aligns with your dreams and values, instead of letting life just happen to you.

RULE 2: REPLACE RESISTANCE WITH PERSISTENCE

Procrastination, doubt, and even fear are typically just habits that once kept you feeling safe. Each time you take even the smallest step forward, you build your self-worth and courage as well as your future success.

RULE 3: SEEK ADVENTURE IN YOUR IDEAS AND EXPERIENCES

Life's most transformative experiences happen when you step beyond familiarity. Pursue the challenges that light a fire in you—whether that's a new goal you conjure up, a physical feat, or an unexpected journey.

RULE 4: FINANCIAL FREEDOM IS A FORM OF SELF-RESPECT

Investing in your future isn't just about security; it's about honoring yourself and the life you want. Create habits now that will let you live with confidence and generosity later.

RULE 5: WISDOM AWAITS THOSE WHO DON'T WHINE

Pain is inevitable but complaining is not. When you engage in the power of reflection, even going over the parts that hurt the most, you learn from mistakes and become truly wise.

RULE 6: PURPOSE EMERGES WHEN YOU ALIGN WITH YOUR WORK

Whether it's the products or services, the processes, the people you serve, or even the test of your fortitude: find meaning and value in what you do. Not every job will have it all, but every job has at least one thing that can help you connect to your purpose.

RULE 7: TAKE CONTROL OF YOUR LEGACY AS YOU LIVE EACH DAY

The way you make others feel will be remembered long after your words and deeds are forgotten. Find ways to leave a positive impression or provide inspiration to other people and contribute in some way to their well-being.

PART I
FACING FEAR

It does not matter how slowly you go
as long as you do not stop.

—Confucius

1

LIONS AND TIGERS AND BEARS – AND THE DOCTOR WILL SEE YOU NOW

The way to develop self-confidence is to do the thing you fear and get a record of successful experiences behind you.

—William Jennings Bryan

Fear. It's the most universal human emotion—and the most misunderstood. Look, I know what you're thinking. You've been told fear keeps you alive, that it's part of your survival instinct. And there's truth to that. Our ancestors needed fear to avoid becoming something else's dinner. Their success is why we can have this conversation now rather than becoming fossil fuel.

But here's what they don't tell you in those inspirational LinkedIn posts: fear in the boardroom isn't protecting you from saber-toothed tigers. It's keeping you from thinking and acting intelligently.

Let me be clear about something. That knot in your stomach when you're about to give your first big presentation? Normal. The hesitation before asking for what you deserve? Human. The voice that whispers you're not ready? We all hear it.

But here's where you're getting tripped up. You've been letting fear drive the car since you were sixteen, with Mom and Dad setting curfews to keep you "safe." You listened to fear when friends offered you questionable substances. You let fear push you to meet deadlines, cram for exams, make the team.

And it worked. Sort of.

But now fear is costing you promotions, relationships, and opportunities. It's making you say things like:

"Maybe I should wait another year before asking for a raise."

"Someone with more experience should lead this project."

"I'll just keep my mouth shut during the meeting."

That's not survival instinct. That's self-sabotage.

Here's a brutal truth no one wants to admit.

Sometimes we use fear as a crutch or a shield. We lean into it. We hide behind it. We stuff our problems in drawers—real or mental—and pretend they don't exist. We avoid difficult conversations, skip doctor's appointments, delay career moves.

You tell yourself you're being practical. Careful. Smart.

You're lying.

Some people pride themselves on confronting what others avoid. Brian Tracy talks about "eating the frog"—doing the most dreaded task first. Sharon Stone tackles the "worst first." These approaches work for those with strong stomach or questionable brain connections, but they're not going to be the go-to answer to the endless challenges you're going to face.

The real antidote to fear isn't bravery or risk-taking. It's not powering through with false confidence or "faking it till you make it."

The cure is developing a healthy relationship with reality.

Start with the facts. When you're afraid to ask for a promotion, what's the real risk? A no? Someone thinking less of you? Or are you actually afraid of finding out you deserve more than you've been settling for? That's shame as much as fear lurking in your brain.

When that project seems overwhelming, break it down. What resources do you need? Who can help? What's the real deadline and the very good (not excellent) outcome you need versus the artificial pressure you're creating?

When you avoid that medical appointment, ask yourself: what's scarier—finding out what's wrong or living with uncertainty and letting things get worse?

Remember Dorothy and her friends on the yellow brick road? They were terrified of lions and tigers and bears. They believed they needed a wizard to give them what they lacked. The real revelation? They already had everything they needed.

So do you.

Fear won't disappear.

It's part of the human operating system. But you can stop letting it drive your decisions. You can recognize it for what it is—a signal, not a stop sign.

Ultimately, facing fear isn't about eliminating it. It's about moving forward with it, until it gets bored because you keep beating it and so it fades away. It's about choosing facts over fiction, action over avoidance, growth over stagnation.

Because in today's corporate jungle, the real predators aren't lions and tigers and bears. They're the opportunities you let fear steal from you. Get the promotion. Get the check-up. Get on with it!

EXERCISE: THE FEAR AUDIT

1. List three decisions you've delayed or avoided in the past 90-days due to fear.
2. For each, write down:
   - The worst-case scenario (what you actually fear)
   - The likely outcome (based on facts, not feelings)
   - The cost of inaction (what you lose by doing nothing)

QUESTION TO REFLECT ON

What would you attempt this week if you knew failure was impossible?

FIRST STEP

Choose one item from your Fear Audit and take the smallest possible action toward it within the next 24 hours. It could be as simple as sending an email, making a phone call, or researching information. The key is to start.

IS FEAR YOUR FRENEMY?

The Guardrail Might Now Be a Roadblock

1

Fear: Your Original Survival App
- Before fear became a sneaky saboteur, it was a reliable, even beloved bodyguard.

- Kept Your Ancestors Alive - *"Maybe don't eat those green berries and steer clear of that volcano."*
- Kept You Out of Trouble - Your parents set curfews not just to ruin your teen years, but to keep you safe.
- Kept You Motivated - Fear of failing pushed you to study, train, or stay on track.
- Kept You From Regret - When something didn't seem in your best interests, you said "no" to bad choices.

> What once helped you navigate life can now hold you back.

2

Fear: From Friend to Foe
- Now fear may have several deceptive personalities that steer you wrong.

- The Anti-motivation Monster: *"You could fail, so let's not even try."*
- The Fretting Failure-monger: *"You need deadline pressure to get started."*
- The Storage Stuffer: *"Just shove this problem in here and pretend it's not a thing."*
- The Cynical Critic: *"Everyone will think you're an idiot."*

> Fear is just a bad habit that you're ready to replace.

3

Fear's Antidote: A Warm Relationship with Reality
- Fear isn't "fixed" by bravery or positive thinking. It's stopped with facts and action.

- Get the real story.
- Run the numbers.
- Talk with a mentor.
- Act intelligently.

> Fear seeks to defeat you. A friend wants the best for you and for you to be your best!

I WAS A "HYPO"

A personal reflection by
John Pierce

Be not afraid of growing slowly, be afraid only of standing still.
—Chinese Proverb

In 1999, I was tagged as a "hypo" in corporate. No, not a hypochondriac. A high potential.

On the good news front, I was awarded an external coach to help me reach that potential.

On the bad news front, I felt immense internal pressure to live up to the label. I thought, "I've got to win. I've got to be number one." I felt an incessant need to push and drive and win. All because the corporate powers above me put a label on me.

In fact, what I've learned over the course of 30 years with my coach, now a dear friend, is that being labeled as high potential is not truly about you. It's meant to describe what you can do for the organization.

When you get over what anyone calls you—high potential, low potential, a winner, a loser, whatever—you gain an awareness of what YOU think of yourself. And, when you define yourself and use the resources you're given or can acquire, then you can shape your career so it reflects what you think is meaningful and productive for you.

If you're labeled high potential in your organization or otherwise feel like there's a lot of expectations about your performance—don't feel like you're cursed, or that you must do this on your own. No one magically reaches their potential without some support. You need a plan. You need new skills. You also need to stop clinging to your old beliefs about yourself. And most likely, you need to admit you need help to take the right actions. Seek out coaching, mentoring, and guidance.

Think about pro athletes and what they must do at each level of their career. Rookie? Try to avoid silly mistakes and fumbles. Mid-career pro? Stay sharp and train hard. Veteran? Maximize your playing years by focusing on your strengths and staying healthy. Every one of these pros has a coach, a trainer, a manager, an agent, and more. You need at least one other person on your side who can help you at this stage of your career.

So, what's your next move? If you really are high potential, acknowledge your flaws. Tackle them systematically. As you gain strengths and skills, you should see more opportunities. When you produce more, you can earn more—more money, more choices, more power or stability.

For me, having high potential evolved into what I could do to help others—specifically people who are struggling in the generation coming up in corporate. From that perspective, I view everyone as having high potential. Some of us have talents that are less obvious or yet unmined, and we need a mentor or coach to unleash that talent. You might think, like I do, that achieving your full potential including unlocking the potential in others.

In my last role, I hired a lot of young, raw, talented people into roles that my peers and my boss kind of scratched their heads and said, "I'm not really sure they're ready." Well, you know what? I wasn't ready in 1999 either, but someone gave me a chance. It's easy for those who've already made it to forget how important new blood is in an organization or the industry.

So be on the lookout for the boss or mentor who does see your potential or who can make an introduction or connection for you. Then, show them what a good choice they made when they chose you!

2

ARE YOU CURSED WITH THE LABEL OF "HIGH POTENTIAL"?

He who fears he will suffer already suffers because he fears.
—Michel de Montaigne

Let's talk about that backhanded compliment you keep getting: "You have so much potential."

The sting comes later, doesn't it? When you're alone with your thoughts, wondering what gap they see between who you are and who they think you should be. That word—potential—starts to feel less like a compliment and more like a judgment.

I see that look in your eyes. That mix of pride and frustration when someone calls you "high potential." It's the same look I've seen in countless young managers who wonder why they're not further along. They fear never getting where they could go and that fear can manifest in some career limiting habits—like self-sabotage.

You might not say it out loud, but I know what you're thinking:

- "Why am I stuck in this job when I'm smarter than my boss?"
- "How did that guy get promoted while I'm still waiting?"
- "When will people recognize what I can really do?"

These thoughts are your "grudge talk"—the soundtrack of self-doubt that plays on repeat in your mind. Left unchecked, it breeds resentment, jealousy, and the kind of self-sabotage that keeps you exactly where you don't want to be.

Here's the brutal truth about potential: It's nothing.

You can't deposit potential in your bank account. You can't use it as a down payment on a house. It's an intangible space between your current reality and some imagined future state of your life that may never be realized.

Think about pro athletes. All of them filled with potential for greatness beyond their current performance. Even those who sign multi-million dollar contracts have coaches. Rookies get coached to channel their raw talent. Veterans get coached to maximize what they have left. And those at the peak of their careers? They get coached to push the upper limit.

The difference between potential and achievement? Simple. It's what you do when you're tired of waiting for recognition and start building the skills you need.

This is where coaching comes in. Not the feel-good, "you're amazing" kind. I mean the real work of examining your beliefs, patterns, and habits that keep you stuck. The kind of guidance that helps you see choices you're missing and strategies you're ignoring.

When I was a Managing Director at Merrill Lynch, I was labeled "high potential." I thought I knew everything—I was a voracious learner, fiercely independent, and convinced I could figure it all out myself.

Then I met Fran Johnston, founder and CEO of Teleos Leaders. She is the coach who changed my trajectory. Working with Fran showed me what I couldn't see on my own: my blind spots, my patterns of self-sabotage, and most importantly, the specific steps I needed to take to close the gap between potential and performance.

The lesson? You can either resent being called "high potential" or you can use it as fuel. But you can't do it alone.

The gap between potential and performance isn't bridged by wishing, complaining, or waiting. It's built through deliberate action, constant learning, and sometimes, accepting help from those who can see what you can't.

EXERCISE: THE POTENTIAL REALITY CHECK

1. Write down three areas where others see your "potential"
2. List the specific skills or behaviors needed to realize each one
3. Rate yourself (1-10) on each skill
4. Identify your lowest two scores—these are your starting points

QUESTION TO REFLECT ON

When have you used potential as an excuse instead of a catalyst for action?

FIRST STEP

Find someone who excels in one of your low-scoring areas. Schedule a 30-minute conversation to learn about their journey from potential to performance. Ask them: "What was the one skill or habit that made the biggest difference?"

IT IS NOT THE MOUNTAIN WE CONQUER BUT OURSELVES.

—SIR EDMUND HILLARY

Are You Cursed with the Label
HIGH POTENTIAL?

1
It Doesn't Feel Like a Compliment

Being called "high potential" can feel like an insult unless you're living up to it. It implies there's a gap between where you are and where you should be.

2
Are You "Grudge Talking?"

- "I'm better than this job."
- "I'm smarter than my boss."
- "How come I earn less than my buddy who doesn't have half the brains I do?"

3
Potential Is Nothing Without Action

- STOP clinging to old beliefs
- ADMIT you need help
- Take action & BUILD new skills
- Seek COACHING & guidance

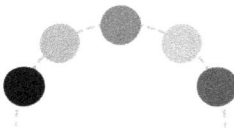

4
Lessons from Pro Athletes

- ROOKIES: Avoid silly mistakes
- MID-CAREER PROS: Stay sharp & train hard
- VETERANS: Maximize strengths & savvy

5
What's Your Next Move?

If You REALLY ARE "High Potential"... Act Like It!
- ✓ Invest in Your Growth
- ✓ Produce More to Earn More
- ✓ Find Your Flaws
- ✓ Tenaciously Tackle Them!

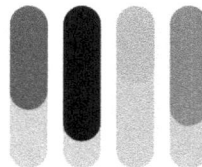

IT'S ALWAYS SWEATY IN PHILADELPHIA

A personal reflection by

Ryan Hall

<small>MUSIC INDUSTRY EXECUTIVE</small>

Working in the music industry is hard, but hot yoga is harder. There's one thing that a 15-year career in the "biz" and almost just as long of a yoga practice has taught me:

The key to growth is the exploration of your edge, the practice of staying when things get uncomfortable. These are the moments when a true breakthrough, an opportunity to learn and to grow, waits just over the horizon. As Baron Baptiste, the founder of Baptiste Power Yoga says, "when we choose our comfort zone over growth, we get stuck."

When I look back at my career, and what it took to get me to where I am today, this message rings true above all else. It's the one lesson I find I repeat most to junior members of my team who may need a word of encouragement early in their professional lives.

Let me back up a second and explain where I'm coming from.

Over the years, I've worn many hats in the music industry. I first got my start as a talent-buyer at a local venue, where I'd book acts to play a weekly Wednesday Locals Night. I'd scour the internet for bands I liked and invite them to come play. I'd then put in the sweat equity to help the bands promote the shows, online, via flyers around the city, handing them out after shows, you get the deal.

Want another fun fact? I lived two hours away from the venue at the time, and my commute consisted of a mix of public transportation and biking in the dead of the humid Philadelphia summers, so getting to the shows each week was quite literally a sweaty ordeal. My boss wasn't the most supportive, more often than not the shows wouldn't sell too well, and I'd head home late at night with another two-hour sweaty commute ahead of me.

It wasn't glamorous, but it was a start.

From there I became a booking agent, both working for a boutique agency as well as starting my own side gig booking friend's bands on East Coast and Midwest tours to small venues around the country.

My days were long and filled with endless cold calling and emailing, trying to convince bars in Detroit why they should even consider booking an Indie Rock band from Philly who didn't have a single fan in the market. It was tiring but it taught me persistence and the value of a strong elevator pitch. I will admit, I sometimes would tread the fine line of truthfulness… *"yes of course they will be able to draw at least 30 people, no problem!"* but I knew the risk was worth the reward. I'd also seen the other side of it in my last role as the one answering the phone at the venue, so I knew how to speak with these people. I was kind and took the extra effort to get to know the person on the other end, their personal lives outside of work, I built relationships that mattered.

The cold emails were brutal, but my network was finally starting to grow.

During all of this, I also started managing some local groups in the Electronic Dance Music scene. My goal at the time was to work in electronic music. I was enamored by the underground rave scene and the community of people it took to sustain it. To achieve this goal, I made it a mission to connect with anyone and everyone in the Philly music scene who even remotely touched this world. That meant even more cold reach outs. If I saw your name attached to a Facebook event for an upcoming concert, you better bet I'd be in your inbox asking to grab a coffee or offering to get involved.

I slowly built a name for myself. The value of being in a smaller city like Philadelphia, compared to the massive hubs of Los Angeles and New York, is that you can realistically get your arms around the industry here, it is manageable to get exposure to all the big players in the space.

I used my contacts from talent-buying and booking to get free tickets and went out to as many shows as I could at night. I was the person standing outside of the club afterwards handing you a flyer for the next show, and people in the scene started to recognize my face. I was never too nervous to ask for backstage passes and soon became a staple in the green room, building relationships with everyone from the box office to the bouncers.

People in roles I admired saw I was working hard and wanted to lift me up as a result.

Shortly thereafter, I attracted the attention of a local management company which was being run by a major group in the Jam Band scene called the Disco Biscuits. The management company was run by some execs at Live Nation and other serious music and artistic organizations in the city.

I'll never forget it, when I first started working for them, my boss at the time told me outright: "Don't expect this job to be one where we tell you exactly what to do. We're not going to handhold you. We see something promising in you, and will help open the doors you need, all you have to do is ask. This job is going to be exactly whatever YOU decide to make of it."

Say no more… I took that directive and ran with it. The next two years with that management company were some of the most formative years of my career. I worked late hours. Experienced more shows and festivals than I could count. I made mistakes. Probably sent some emails I shouldn't have. But I learned so much.

I learned that to succeed, I needed to be given the freedom to fail.

From that experience, my career really took off. I ended up taking a job at a Music Marketing Agency at the time when social media was just getting started. I was the 10th hire at a new startup where every day was a new adventure. Every day was a new chance to fail.

I didn't know it then, but I was starting myself off on a path that would define the next 10 years of my career, one that would take me deep into the world of digital marketing. Everything I had been doing up until that point set me up perfectly for this world. I like to call digital marketing "the crossroads of the music industry". Every sector of the business interacts with a digital marketer at some point, from booking agents to artist managers, record labels, publicists, and artists themselves. My cursory experience in all those areas made me the prime specimen for the role, as I knew how to speak the language of each stakeholder and achieve their objective.

I rose quickly in the ranks and soon was the digital marketing lead for some of the biggest artists in the world, executing social media campaigns for the likes of Alicia Keys, Gwen Stefani, Janet Jackson, Celine Dion, and more. I moved to New York to start a new life and was frequently traveling between LA, Nashville, and London for client meetings.

With lots of success also comes lots of stress, and these years were some of the most uncomfortable times in my career. The 10-person agency I joined had grown to over 100 people in five years. I was managing a team of 14 people under me and constantly having to navigate times of being overloaded, learning how to balance an ever-growing client list. There were times when I felt I couldn't possibly manage one more thing, add one more spinning plate to the mix, but time and time again I surprised myself. Through believing in myself, I was able to achieve more than I ever imagined.

I stayed when things were uncomfortable, I knew there was always a breakthrough on the horizon.

To bring it back to the metaphor that started this whole thing, some of the best yoga classes I've taken were the hardest. They're tough, sweaty, and put you in positions that sometimes make you want to run away. But if you stick it out, you realize that you're not alone. There's a room full of students going through the same struggle, and a teacher at the front who wants you to succeed but leaves you with just enough room to fail. In these moments you find that a real breakthrough is waiting for you, to show you what you're really made of, if only you'll wait and see what it has to offer.

ABOUT RYAN HALL

Ryan Hall has 15 years of music industry experience in digital marketing, artist management, and touring. Growing up in Philadelphia, he started out as a booking agent and talent buyer for local venues. Eventually he joined a management company, Aorta management, where he fostered the growth of hip hop and dance music artists throughout the Philadelphia and New York City area. In 2013 he turned his focus toward digital marketing, becoming one of the early team members at Fame House, helping grow the company and leading to an eventual acquisition by Universal Music Group. While there, Ryan led full scale digital marketing campaigns for dozens of artists and brands, including Alicia Keys, Phantogram, ODESZA, Robin Schulz, Corona, Toni Braxton, DJ Carnage, and more. Ryan's work on marketing campaigns led to four years of back-to-back Music Ally Sandbox awards, which identified these campaigns as amongst the best music marketing campaigns of the year, as well as 2 Webby awards. After Fame House, he led the social team at Weller Media Agency, growing their client roster and overseeing a team of 14 social marketers, ensuring that clients and teams are on the cutting edge of digital marketing trends. There he oversaw campaigns for Live Nation, Celine Dion, Gwen Stefani, to name a few. He most recently has returned to his roots at Fame House to launch a new department called Community & Content. There he and his team consult artists on how to grow and engage communities of superfans, turning fans from passive listeners to lifelong supporters.

3

WHAT REJECTION SAYS TO RATIONAL PEOPLE

Success is not final, failure is not fatal:
it is the courage to continue that counts.

—Winston Churchill

D o you take rejection personally?

Of course you do. Most people do. But here's the thing about rejection—it's as inevitable as the sunset and as impersonal as gravity.

You don't rage at the Earth for rotating away from the sun. You don't blame yourself when it rains on your picnic. Yet when someone says "no" to you at work, you act like the universe is specifically targeting you. Feels like you've been shut out. Shut down. Told to shut up.

Let me set the record straight: rejection is just another event in your day.

It's like traffic or weather. It's a moment in time that signals the end of one thing and the beginning of something else. Nothing more.

The real problem isn't rejection. It's your belief that you should control everything in your life. Everything in your career. Everything that happens in a company you work for. It's a killer fear to believe that somehow the decisions made about you or what you want are reflections of your worth as a human being.

They're not.

Here's what rejection actually is: someone is solving their problem without you. You are not in their equation. What are they calculating? The only thing on their mind is how to protect or advance their interests, their project, their budget, their reputation. If you're not included, you're merely collateral damage in their decision-making process.

Does that make it fair? No. Does it make it rational? Rarely. But it's the reality of corporate life.

When you get passed over for a promotion, denied a project, or let go from a position, the person making that decision isn't judging your soul. They're making a business calculation—often a short-sighted one—based on their immediate needs.

The dangerous part comes when you take their decision and make it your truth.

When you start telling yourself stories about what their choice means about your value. When you connect this rejection to past disappointments and create a narrative that you're somehow broken or unworthy. Like you're looking at stars in the sky and seeing a constellation and you believe they collaborated to form the shape of a lion or the big dipper.

Stop.

Rational people understand that work is a gamble, and the house always wins. Companies will protect themselves first, always. Your five, ten, or twenty years of loyalty mean little when quarterly numbers are down. Your past performance or future projections matter less than today's profit margin.

This isn't cynicism—it's reality.

So how do you transform rejection from a crushing blow to a constructive pivot?

First, recognize it for what it is: information, not condemnation. Someone made a decision based on their needs, not your worth.

Second, keep moving. Literally. Make calls, send emails, have coffee with industry contacts. Motion creates momentum, and momentum creates opportunities.

Third, expand your horizon. Rejection often reveals the limits of where you've been looking. Reach out to people you admire but haven't connected with yet. Start saying YES to all the opportunities you were unwilling to invest in previously. Get uncomfortable saying YES. Attend events you've avoided. Prospect in unfamiliar territories.

Fourth, feed your mind and soul. Fill your head with positive voices, whether through books, podcasts, or conversations. Balance the noise of rejection with the clarity of inspiration.

Fifth and finally, serve. Find a way to use your talents to help others. Volunteer, mentor, teach. People, pets, a community planting a neighborhood garden or cleaning up a playground. It's hard to feel worthless when you're actively making a difference.

Remember: rejection is just one sunset. Night will follow, then dawn, then another day. The person who rejected you will move on. You should too.

EXERCISE: THE REJECTION REFRAME

1. Write down your most recent rejection.
2. List three emotions you felt.
3. Now rewrite the situation as if it were happening to someone else—someone you care about.
4. What advice would you give them?
5. Apply that advice to yourself.

QUESTION TO REFLECT ON

What opportunities might be waiting in the space
that rejection just created in your life?

FIRST STEP

Identify one person who has transformed rejection into success in your industry. Research their story and find one specific action they took that you will implement this week.

FAILURE, FORGIVENESS, AND FREEDOM ON THE ROAD TO SUCCESS

A personal reflection by

Tony Sirianni

PUBLISHER AND OWNER OF ADVISORHUB

You have power over your mind—not outside events.
Realize this, and you will find strength.

—Marcus Aurelius

The unvarnished truth is rougher than you imagine. Finding the great in a great recession takes a toll.

Comebacks, like overnight sensations (that are typically 20 years in the making), fail to tell the truth about the zig-zagging road trip(s) that lead to them. No one outside of the travel-worn trekker knows the work, hardship, endless effort, and pure luck involved in making it. The rise and fall and rise again to success can be inspiring, if you're the audience. But, when it's your comeback story: the grit never scrapes out cleanly from under your fingernails, the callouses never buff away, and the rod and pins holding you together still rattle.

Comebacks, by their very nature, are born in failure. So, it's only the very human trait of denial to blame when a magnetic success story overlooks the credit due to the main character: failure. Without failure's central contribution, the beloved comeback story cannot be told. Hence, I may shock you when I tell you mine without power washing the truth from it.

The Great Recession was like living through a slow motion trainwreck. I was dead center, but somehow didn't think that I would be a casualty. I was accustomed to being in the middle of crises, through bad markets and bubbles. I had led groups of financial advisors and clients through the worst that markets throw at us. As a financial complex manager, managing one of the largest retail brokerage complexes in the country, I felt that it was during a crisis that I truly earned my pay.

Shutting Off on the Way to Shutting Down

My hubris, historical resilience, and my ability to compartmentalize were elements of the brew that made reality go out of focus for me. I simply did not "think" it possible that Smith Barney would go out of business, even as my presence at the firm was a testament to the formerly unthinkable idea that Legg Mason retail, where I had been a rising executive, would ever be sold. Yet, it had been (more specifically horse-traded) to a rival. So, I had lived experience that the unthinkable was worth thinking and planning for.

It took a while for me to understand that my career was built on trust and belief in a system that was not constructed for trustworthiness. It took me a long time to realize that my career, based on that system, was never in my control.

Beliefs die hard even in the face of harder realities. In my case, the numbers told the story that I did not want to hear. My seven-figure compensation plan was cut fivefold, even as I was given more responsibility. My equity positions, my life's savings, mostly in the firm's deferred comp plan stock, dwindled from millions that guaranteed a solid retirement to an amount that enabled me to pay for my children's private school tuition for precisely one year.

Concurrently, the housing crisis led the buyer of my "old" house to walk away at closing. That happened the day after I had closed and moved into my "new" house. I was long (meaning, I was in debt for) $3.5 million in real estate exactly at the time my income declined sharply. Things would improve as they always had, right? Right? Wrong. Wrong.

No Degree of Safety

The excruciating details of being the parent of four children during this time are probably too awful to hear so they won't bear repeating. I'll leave it in a quick streaming of consciousness: humility is a great teacher, short sales, food stamps, hungry kids, burning furniture for heat, selling cherished valuables, pawning watches, foregoing medical treatments, and washing cars for tips, while pondering the value of a law and master's degrees can test a person's mettle.

Turning things around required something I did not expect. All the hard work, belief, and effort in the world would not bring back my old job. Nothing would bring back the world as I knew it. Turning around isn't the right term. Turning off the old beliefs in companies and systems so I could rely on myself to create something completely different is what it took.

I certainly don't wish financial collapse on anyone, and for sure dealing with medical crises is worse, but while losing everything can be a dark journey: the stark reality of unalterable change and the lessons it taught were also the breeding ground for success.

The First Thing I Had To Do Was Forgive

Forgiveness was an awakening. It lifted every burden and honed my purpose. I was taking business failures that were beyond my control way too personally. A fundamental truth was that the people who ran Legg Mason, Smith Barney, and Morgan Stanley were not out to get me. They had their own problems.

The people who were closer to me—the ones who said my name regularly during the good times—that was personal. Cheated by partners, abandoned by my social groups, ignored by people I thought were friends, I slowly realized that I was on my own to fix my family's future. That was a blessing.

To move forward, I had to let the past go. But that past wasn't going anywhere until I forgave everyone and everything, including myself.

Forgiveness paved the way to re-invention, and from re-invention to re-building my life better. With no seven figure retail jobs around, and car wash tips not cutting it, I set out to invent a career that used my skill sets and experience.

The Long Road Back to the Future

I was the only person I knew who had been both a managing director at three wirehouses and a founder of two-multibillion-dollar RIA firms. Building RIAs is rewarding because it's strategic and challenging, but the ramp up is not a fast financial homerun. Creating RIA wealth is a long game. Over time, by standing up two very successful RIA firms and retaining my founder's shares, I put myself in the position to participate in their long-term success. That enabled me to create something new.

My master's degree is in creative writing, not economics. So, when the opportunity to buy AdvisorHub came up, I jumped on it.

Here's the Comeback You Waited For

We transformed AdvisorHub from a salacious blog to the number one news site for financial advisors. My consulting business continued to grow and my clients became customers across multiple business lines. During COVID we launched a dual cover, first of its kind, print magazine that, bucking recent trends, has been profitable since day one.

AdvisorHub became a springboard for advisor-focused advocacy and complimentary business lines. We created a "1,000 Advisors to Watch" list with a different set of criteria from old media lists. Our events business has been selling out since inception, and we have permanently reshaped coverage of news in our space. AdvisorHub is at the center of change in our business. That's a huge lesson from my story.

I no longer feel that change is somehow destroying the things I love.

I now know change offers opportunity.

I feel that I am an agent of change in a positive way, not just for myself but for the industry I love.

I'm now in a position, with some new partners in my consulting business, to be able to offer the type of RIA financing I could only have dreamed of when I started my two firms. Helping firms grow with advice as well as capital partnership is opening new horizons and broad vistas for growth.

I've learned to be a partner with change, seeing myself as a positive transformative partner in success. I no longer fear change. I no longer deny the need for it. A re-invention mindset spurs creativity and allows for critical adjustments and crystal-clear vision.

If I am not afraid of change, then I do not need to look away from reality.

Change and grappling with elements beyond my control shaped the most difficult period of my life, but the ability to forgive was in my control all along.

Choosing forgiveness over blame created the avenues for growth.

The simple fact was that had I not lost everything, I would not have tried to do anything great. For me re-invention came at great cost. But giving forgiveness was free.

Even better, forgiveness gave me freedom.

ABOUT TONY SIRIANNI

Tony Sirianni is a 29-year financial services industry veteran and the publisher/owner of Advisor Hub, the nation's leading financial services news website. He is the Managing Partner of Sirianni Strategy Group, former President of Steward Partners Consulting Solutions, and founding partner of both Steward Partners Holdings and Washington Wealth Management (CEO), two of the fastest growing RIAs in history. He was an Executive Director and Complex Manager at Morgan Stanley, Smith Barney, and Legg Mason. He ran a bank brokerage program at Crestar bank in its Richmond headquarters, was Director of Annuities for Mass Mutual Insurance in Virginia, ran an internal wholesaling team for Oppenheimer Funds at the World Trade Center, and was a broker at Merrill Lynch on 5th Ave. in Manhattan.

Tony has been roundly acknowledged by the financial press as an innovator and thought leader in the emerging post-wirehouse advisor world. He turned AdvisorHub from a salacious blog, into the most respected advisor news site on the street. His innovative publishing ideas like AH's Deals and Comp pages, RIA Center, Recruiting Wire, Enforcement section, and more are much copied by competitors. He holds seminars for marketing execs and advertising firms on mega-trends in the advisor marketplace. His opinion articles are known to drive policy decisions at major firms. He has created the industry's top culture survey, and the Industry in Transition event, an annual sold-out advisor and industry leader event in NYC that brings hundreds of the top advisors in the country together to hear from C-suite leadership. He is a sought-after speaker on industry trends and challenges. His podcast attracts leaders of the nation's largest advisor firms as guests of his one-on-one interviews.

4

IN EVERY BRAVE LIFE,
YOU FIND A GREAT MENTOR

Picture the moment your chest tightens before making a career-defining presentation. Now imagine having someone in your corner who's faced that exact fear—and survived. Even thrived.

That's a mentor.

Fear doesn't disappear when you find a mentor. They can't wave a magic wand and make your anxiety about that upcoming board meeting vanish. They can't make a product launch go without a hitch. What they can do is far more valuable: help you see your fear for what it really is—not a stop sign, but a signal.

Most people think mentors are there to give advice or open doors. Wrong. A true mentor's greatest gift is showing you how they face their own fears. They reveal that the confidence you admire in them wasn't built on fearlessness, but on moving forward despite the fear. Sometimes with the fear. They didn't wait until the fear disappeared to take action, so they can show you how to live with it.

What happens when you reveal your fear to a great mentor?

They don't say, "just get over it." They'll ask you what's really at stake. Is it your reputation? Your job? Your self-image? They'll help you separate the real risks from the imaginary monsters your mind creates at 3 AM.

They won't minimize your fear. They'll share their own. That presentation they gave that changed their career? They threw up before walking on stage. That risky decision that made their reputation? They lost sleep for weeks. They'll show you that fear isn't proof you're weak—it's proof you're human.

They won't solve your problems for you. They'll ask questions that expose the faulty logic feeding your fear. "What's the worst that could happen?" isn't just a cliché—it's a tool for dismantling anxiety. When you answer honestly, you often find the worst case isn't as catastrophic as you imagined. A worst case exists, for sure, even if it's not the exaggerated version you're using to terrorize yourself. But there's odds of failure and success that a mentor can help you ascertain so you make a considered (not fearful) decision.

Most importantly, they won't let you use fear as an excuse. They'll share how they pushed through similar moments, not to shame you, but to show you it's possible. They'll remind you that regret lasts longer than embarrassment, and that playing it safe is often the riskiest move of all.

Finding this kind of mentor requires vulnerability.

You need someone who's climbed the mountain you're facing and can tell you, "Yes, it's scary getting up here, but the view is worth it." Look for someone who's failed publicly and recovered. Someone who admits their mistakes without losing their authority. Someone who can laugh at their past fears without dismissing yours.

When you find them, don't waste their time pretending you're fearless. Show up with your real fears:

- "I'm afraid I'll be exposed as a fraud in this new role."
- "I'm terrified of confronting my underperforming team member."
- "I'm scared to ask for the resources I need to succeed."

A great mentor won't fix these fears. They'll help you face them. They'll show you how they've turned similar fears into fuel for growth. They'll remind you that everyone in that boardroom has felt exactly what you're feeling—the difference between stalling and succeeding is what they did next.

The irony? Finding a mentor requires facing one of our deepest fears: asking for help. But that first act of courage—reaching out to someone you admire and saying, "I need guidance"—is often the beginning of transforming fear from a barrier into a catalyst.

Because in the end, a mentor doesn't teach you to be fearless. They teach you to be brave.

Oh, one more thing: all mentors are not great mentors.

Watch out for self-serving behaviors. If you see something that makes you uncomfortable, use your common sense. Are you avoiding a difficult topic or do you need to bring a close to this relationship and find someone truly in your corner? Remember, you are seeking a great mentor.

EXERCISE: THE FEAR-SHARING FRAMEWORK

1. List your three biggest career fears.
2. Identify what each fear is protecting (ego, comfort, status quo).
3. Write down what facing each fear could teach you.
4. Choose one to share with a potential mentor.

QUESTION TO REFLECT ON

What fear have you been hiding that a mentor could help you face?

FIRST STEP

Draft an email to a potential mentor that includes one specific fear you're facing and asks for 30 minutes of their time to discuss how they've handled similar situations. Be clear: you're not looking for solutions, but for perspective on facing this fear.

THE POWER OF MENTORSHIP

Unlocking Confidence and Career Success with the Right Guide

1

Why Mentors Matter

The Right Mentor is Magic

- Mentors **accelerate growth** by providing insight and feedback.
- They help **navigate career challenges** and sharpen decision-making.
- Mentors **expand your network** and open new opportunities.

2

Qualities of a Great Mentor

5 Essential Skills

Experience – Proven track record in their field

Empathy – Understanding & supportive

Honesty – Truthful, constructive feedback

Challenging – Expects struggle *and* success

Consistency – Reliable and long-term guidance

3

How to Find the Right Mentor

3 Steps to Secure the Right Mentor

Identify Leaders You Admire – Observe individuals with qualities you respect

Build Relationships – Engage through networking and offer value in return

Ask for Guidance – Listen to leaders with their potential for mentoring you in mind

4

Impact of Mentorship on Career Growth

Measurable Benefits of Having a Mentor

"Mentees were **promoted 5 times more often** than those not mentored."

"25% of mentored employees **increased their salary**, compared with 5% of employees who did not participate."

Source: Mentorloop

5

Who Have Been Your Greatest Mentors?

Shout Out to Your Mentors

Tag your mentors and share some of the key advice, ideas, or support they provided to you!

THE CYCLE OF MENTORING LEADS TO ENDLESS GAINS

A personal reflection by

Phil Waxelbaum

FOUNDER AND CEO, MASADA CONSULTING, LLC

I have spent a blessed career engaged in the cycle of mentoring. It is the principal driver of success and joy in my work.

On my first day as a financial advisor, volunteer mentors overwhelmed me. Their outreach to me was well-meaning, but filtering down the choices to someone I could bet my early career on was a tough task. I think mostly I got lucky with my choice. Over several years, one man became my sounding board as well as my cheerleader. I say sounding board because mentorship is a two-way street. You must put effort into assessing advice and how to act on it.

Mentoring is more like a funnel of decisions, one leading to another until an action step is clear and compelling. Mentoring is not a "do as you are told" exercise. In fact, a great mentor gives you room to explore and do your own discovery. They gently bump you on the right path but allow you to make mistakes while you are learning what's right for you.

It is a lot like quality parenting. Scraped knees are acceptable but let's avoid broken bones. I did lots of knee scraping. The results were wonderful.

The biggest challenge in my early success was self-doubt. Was I succeeding because I was good or because my mentor was a genius? I still don't know but as time passes it stops mattering. My success as an advisor led me to a path in management. Because I was a product of mentorship, I was better equipped than most.

However, a new role required a new mentor. Lucky again as I was pulled under the wing of the company president. Lucky is an understatement. He had done it all with obviously great success. I kicked into high gear as a mentee, gaining a career's worth of knowledge in five blazing years. That chapter of mentorship resulted in rapid promotion and ultimately a board seat. Fairytale like.

What I didn't realize at the time is my success lifted my mentor as well. He kept helping me because my results were his results. I didn't stall and he never stopped helping even decades after his retirement and I had moved on to a new affiliation. Still, it took a while to regain balance when he was no longer ever present.

One day during a very scary and turbulent time in the business I was lamenting to a colleague how much I missed having a mentor. He responded that perhaps I had missed an obvious fact—that I had matriculated to being mentor myself. He pointed out that I now had a very large flock who saw me as their guide. People whose future careers and lives I could affect positively counted on my insights and support. In return I was now the one that benefited from their success. What a moment of revelation!

By paying forward the gift of mentorship that I had been given, I was now receiving more than ever before. That is why I call it "The Cycle of Mentoring." That is my guiding light as I continue to engage with up-and-coming leaders.

We are all just passing on our best mentor driven experience. Not everyone will receive great mentoring, nor will everyone be able to provide it. However, when you meet your match as a mentor or mentee, it is magic for your career.

ABOUT PHILIP WAXELBAUM

As founder and CEO of Masada Consulting, LLC since 2012, Phil Waxelbaum has been engaged as a retained board consultant to first tier Wall Street firms and as a recruiting consultant to many of the industry's top financial advisors. Phil began his career in the financial services industry as an advisor, and over the next four decades held positions in field leadership, investment banking, national sales management, and head of private client group.

I WOULD HAVE TAKEN BETTER NOTES

A personal reflection by

John Pierce

A gem cannot be polished without friction,
nor a man perfected without trials.

—Seneca

In a broadcast studio somewhere in Los Angeles, California, I'm about to get in front of a microphone and give some folks a piece of my mind. Going to tell my truth (minus most of the curse words) and talk about what "playing by the rules" gets you—and costs you. Let's be honest: your corporate career will probably wring you dry, even while it makes you rich.

The corporate world can catapult you into skyscrapers with corner offices and grant you power that dwarfs what you'd find in a start-up or family business. But make no mistake—it can simultaneously steal your personal vision, erode your self-reliance, and yes, even break your heart. I say this as someone with 30 wildly successful years in financial services who's not only navigated my own path but launched and nurtured hundreds of careers. So, while I may have both love and hate for the game, I've certainly earned my player card.

The renowned therapist Esther Perel titled her podcast, "Where Should We Begin?" Millions tune in for pearls of wisdom or to witness breakthrough moments that transform lives or relationships. It's captivating because you're not the one squirming on the hot seat—you're just a spectator to someone else's catastrophe or salvation.

What's fascinating is that regardless of the issue, the show's title gives guests permission to start anywhere. After all, it asks: "Where should we begin?"

But I think that's a false choice. In those people's lives—and in yours—life has already begun. Some damage has occurred. Some success has, too. Instead of obsessing over where to begin, perhaps we should focus on where we want to end up.

Exactly where are you steering this career of yours? What's the finale you envision? What's your exit strategy? I'm posing these questions whether you're currently basking in achievements, recognition, and compensation—or if you're feeling frustrated, overlooked, or shortchanged.

Here's the reality check: you'll likely navigate two to five distinct careers in your lifetime—with numerous jobs scattered throughout. The person who spends 30 years in the same sector, organization, or role is practically a unicorn these days. Even rarer is someone saying, "Plan how you want this chapter of your working life to conclude. Strategize for what will likely be 50+ years of earning a living."

With three degrees in a file cabinet—bachelor's, master's, and doctorate—you'd think I would have been thoroughly prepared by academia's finest minds. Yet not a single lecture, workshop, or assignment prepared me for the real battlefield of corporate America. Had they done so, I would've been front row, recording every word. Instead, I learned it all the hard way, day after day, decade after decade.

As I map out my next 30 years, my priority is ensuring I help prepare you and other bright talents as you climb the ladder or decide to jump off into something more adventurous. Remember this: building lasting success today begins with keeping the ideal ending in mind. Consider it the corporate version of "start with your obituary and work backwards"—except we're talking about your career, not your life. And trust me, there's a difference—though sometimes corporate makes you forget that.

5

IMAGINE THE END OF YOUR STORY

I'm still standing better than I ever did,
looking like a true survivor, feeling like a little kid.
—Elton John

What scares you more than anything? For most, it's not spiders or public speaking—it's the fear of a wasted life. A fear of failing to accomplish anything meaningful.

We dance around this fear daily. We mask it with smaller concerns that can balloon up to obscure the larger issues. After all, we're hit with metrics that matter in the moment: quarterly targets, approval ratings, that promotion we're chasing. But underneath it all lurks that primal question: "Will my life have meant something when I'm near the end of it?"

Let me tell you something most career books won't: Your greatest fear is also your greatest ally. Actively focusing on the big question, gives you more than perspective. It gives you the guidance system you need to make sense of the daily, weekly, quarterly metrics and decisions.

In business, we've always known this. We start with the end in mind. We craft exit strategies before launching startups. We write vision statements and corporate missions that paint a picture of where we're headed. We create strategic plans that map the journey from here to there.

Why? Because clarity about the destination makes the journey less terrifying.

When you can see your North Star clearly, everything changes.

Here's what happens. Fear becomes contextual rather than existential. When you know where you're headed, today's setback becomes just that—a setback, not a life sentence. That presentation you bombed? That promotion you missed? That project that failed? They're detours, not dead ends. You can say, "This hurts now, but it doesn't change my ultimate goal or destination."

Decisions become easier. Without a clear destination, every fork in the road feels paralyzing. Should you take that transfer? Accept that lateral move? Challenge your boss? When you've defined your end goal, these decisions transform from anxiety-inducing guesswork to strategic calculations.

You simply ask, "Which choice brings me closer to my vision?"

Your resilience deepens. Ever notice how some people bounce back from failure while others collapse? The difference isn't talent or luck—it's purpose. When you're clear about where you're going, rejection or failure becomes information, not indictment. You think, "That approach didn't work; let me try another path" instead of "I'm not good enough."

Distractions lose their power. The corporate world is designed to fracture your attention—endless emails, pointless meetings, office politics. A clear vision acts as a filter, helping you distinguish between what deserves your energy and what's just noise. You develop the confidence to say no to things that don't serve your larger purpose.

Your courage grows naturally. Most career advice tells you to "be brave" without explaining how. The truth is, courage isn't something you find—it's something that finds you when your "why" is bigger than your fear. When you've pictured holding your grandchild while reflecting on a life well-lived, asking for that raise doesn't seem so daunting anymore. Or you've envisioned diving into the surf on a crystal clear day because you traveled to the place of your dreams and you live there, your boss giving you grief is just another moment in a day at work.

Time becomes an ally, not an enemy.

Without a vision, each passing year brings anxiety—another year gone, another opportunity missed. But when you're building toward something meaningful, time works for you. Each experience, even the painful ones, becomes material for your masterpiece rather than evidence of your failure.

Your focus shifts from validation to contribution. Most career frustration stems from seeking external approval. But when you're clear about your ultimate impact, you stop worrying so much about who's noticing your work today and start focusing on its lasting value. This is profoundly liberating.

You develop appropriate detachment. Vision gives you the ability to care deeply about your work without being defined by it. You can pour yourself into projects while maintaining the perspective that this particular job, this particular company, this particular role is just one chapter in your larger story.

Perhaps most importantly, a clear vision allows you to experience joy along the way. When you know you're heading in the right direction, you can appreciate the journey without constant anxiety about whether you're "there" yet. You can celebrate small wins, knowing they're building toward something meaningful.

This is why the most successful people aren't necessarily the most talented, but the most clear-minded. They've faced the ultimate fear—defining what truly matters to them—and in doing so, they've disarmed all the lesser fears that paralyze the rest of us.

So when it comes to your own life, don't wing it.

Why let fear paralyze you instead of propelling you forward at a faster speed? Even while you react to daily fires, make sure you're building toward your personal vision. Never become a passenger in your own story.

Here's the truth: the day will come when you're closer to the end than the beginning. You'll look back and see how you arrived where you landed. The question is: will you be proud of the path you took, or will you wonder why you never charted your own course?

This isn't morbid—it's motivating. When you face the ultimate fear—the finite nature of your time—smaller fears lose their power. Getting rejected for a promotion seems trivial when measured against your life's purpose. Office politics become background noise when you're clear about your more desirable destination.

The fear of failing at your career pales in comparison to the fear of succeeding at the wrong one.

So let's do what scares you.

Let's imagine the end. Picture yourself decades from now, looking back. What will have mattered? What will you wish you'd done? Who will you wish you'd become?

Consider these six dimensions:

1. **Career and Professional Development**: Beyond titles and paychecks, what impact do you want to have made? What problems do you want to have solved? What will you have built that outlasts you?
2. **Financial Stability and Growth**: Not just numbers in accounts, but what freedom will those resources have given you? What securities will you have provided? What opportunities will you have created?
3. **Health and Well-being**: How will you have treated the one body you were given? What experiences will it have carried you through? What habits will have sustained you?
4. **Personal Development and Learning**: What will you have mastered? What wisdom will you have gained? How will your mind have expanded?
5. **Relationships and Social Connections**: Who will stand beside you at the end? Whose lives will be better because you were in them? What love will you have given and received?
6. **Purpose and Contribution**: What mark will you have left on the world? What will live on after you? What will have been your unique contribution?

This exercise isn't about planning every detail—it's about finding your North Star when the fog of fear descends.

When you're crystal clear about your ending, the plot twists along the way—the rejections, the setbacks, the failures—become chapters in your story rather than the end of it. Your current fears shrink when measured against the arc of your life.

The most unshakable confidence comes not from never being afraid, but from knowing your fears are temporary scenes in a much larger story—a story you're authoring.

EXERCISE: THE EULOGY EXERCISE

1. Write your own "celebration of life" as you would want it read at your memorial (after you're 100 years old).
2. Identify the three accomplishments you're most proud of in this imagined future.
3. Note the two biggest regrets you avoided.
4. List the one quality people remembered most about you.

QUESTION TO REFLECT ON

What current fear is stopping you from living out or
moving toward the story you just imagined?

FIRST STEP

Choose one dimension from the six listed above where you feel most out of alignment with your envisioned future. Identify one small action you can take this week that moves you closer to that vision—something so small that fear can't reasonably stop you.

ASSESSMENT

THE PIERCE PROCESS TO
HARNESS FEAR, DREAD, WORRY, AND DOUBT

If they are left running rampant or cycling through your mind, feelings like fear, dread, worry, and doubt can impair your confidence, your clarity, and your sleep. Yet, when you consider that most individuals experience these emotions, it might occur to you that there must be a reason for these four nearly universal elements of the human condition.

The spike of any these feelings, sometimes out of the blue and sometimes in reaction to an event or interaction, is natural. Even when you experience a "near miss," like nearly being hit by a bus when you step off the curb, it's natural to feel a wave of fear after the fact—even though you clearly survived the incident. The rush of adrenalin tells the brain to "make sense of this feeling!" So, the brain, in this case the amygdala, which is a primal part of your anatomy, does the work. Thus, fear is the result. You might develop a longer-term fear of buses or walking across the street from that one incident. You might even develop a more generalized anxiety like hypervigilance whenever you are not in control of a situation.

Often, we've relied on negative emotions to act as guardrails—to keep us safe or on track. As teenagers, we don't stay out all night because we dread facing parents who either will be angry or concerned. So, we might have learned that fear is a good thing to have, because it keeps us safe from their yelling or crying.

In general, fear, dread, worry, and doubt are oddly useful. They ignite our desire to chill, procrastinate, delay, and indulge in something more fun than getting work done. They help us use the clock for motivation rather rely on our own will power, because when the deadline is looming (tik, tik, tik) most of us sit down and do the work. Deadlines are often an easier guardian to obey than self-discipline is to generate.

You may rely on one of these four emotions more than the others. It becomes a default reasoning or reflexive habit you use in lots of situations. For example, perhaps you drive close to the speed limit because you fear getting a speeding ticket. Someone else might speed but worry about getting caught, so they are vigilant about looking for police cars on the road. Either one will keep you awake on a long drive!

So, if we're being realistic, we can accept that even the worst emotions have helped us stay on track, get things done, and perhaps even be better employees, bosses, family members, friends, and citizens.

Now, before you decide to just live with fear, dread, worry, and doubt, consider how you could take the lessons you've learned from them and live well—without all the negativity. After all some of these negative emotions are just old habits that you have outgrown (you probably don't have a curfew anymore). And some are distorting the reality that you truly need to grasp, with all the possibilities that are inherent in at least a little uncertainty, as you plan for your future. Any one of them could be stealing your vitality, optimism, and energy.

Imagine having the self-motivation, self-discipline, and confidence that produces great outcomes, without all the misery and sleeplessness!

That's what this 10-step process will help you accomplish.

The following questions and your responses will help you learn from your past, distinguish between irrational fears and likely realities, explore how fear can be a useful tool in preparing for challenges, and see how you might turn fear into a positive influence in crafting your responses and actions.

Remember: Always start with a specific fear, dread, worry, or doubt. Take a moment to clearly articulate what it is that you'd like to address or change. Then, put it in the form of a question.

Examples:

You may choose something simple to identify that has been with you a long time, like:

What will I do if I encounter a snake or spider?

Or you might feel motivated to tackle something related to work, like:

Will I be able to handle a deadline for the project that's due next week?

You might even be ready to take on a bigger topic, like:

What will happen if my company gets acquired and I'm not chosen by the new ownership?

Here's the process.

1 What specifically is the fear, dread, worry, or doubt? Write it as a question, just like you see in the examples.

2 How is this emotion showing up in your life or work? What is its impact on you, your motivation, productivity, or well-being?

③ How does this emotion help you on the issue? What does it stop you from doing, keep you doing, or spur you to plan or devise?

④ What do you like about the result? Does it help you excuse yourself from situations you don't enjoy? Does it allow you to engage in something you enjoy more? Does it give you something to discuss with friends?

⑤ What about the feeling do you NOT enjoy? Write down a comprehensive list.

⑥ What would you do if you discarded the feeling? How would you go about your work or life differently? What would change for you? What would improve, be easier, or lighter?

7 What would be more difficult if you discarded the feeling?

8 What feeling would you choose as a substitute? For example, would you choose relaxed, easy-going, cooperative, assertive, content, agreeable, open, curious, or strong?

9 Choose your new feeling and write a statement that answers your question. For example, "If I felt relaxed about (issue), then I would _____."

10 Now, imagine doing exactly what you wrote. How would you feel when you were doing it? How would you feel about yourself afterward? What would you learn about yourself?

Great job! Now you're ready to put it into practice. And you can take on each negative feeling with the exact same process to conquer and vanquish it.

ASSESSMENT

THE PIERCE LIFE JOURNEY MAP

Are you an "on-course" person or an "of course" person? You can intentionally drive your life "on course" rather than submissively react with "of course" when events happen to you. Will you make choices every day that lead you to your goals and live a vibrant, ambitious life? Or, will you find yourself almost sleepwalking through life, getting what you've always gotten? Now is the time to choose.

On Course

For ambitious, visionary, self-motivated people, this life journey map is quite literally a dream come true. When you live "on course," you keep your dreams in mind every day. You make decisions and choices *before* events, opportunities, obstacles, and people show up in your life. With this type of imaginative planning, you know how to take action when anticipated or unexpected things arise.

Of Course

Most people live a "groundhog day" kind of existence, where, of course, the same types of things—including bad luck—keep happening to them. If you are routinely reacting automatically to your life, of course, you get the same results. That's how people wind up feeling stalled, overlooked, or unfulfilled.

Had enough? Let's get on course!

This Pierce Life Journey Map will guide you to reflect on your long-term goals, interim milestones, potential pitfalls, and strategies to kickstart a new perspective and accelerate your progress in six key dimensions of life Career, Finance, Health, Personal Development, Relationships, and Purpose. The map will set you on course to achieve what you want and provide a mechanism for accountability, as well as pivot points to make changes as your journey unfolds.

Instructions

Follow the directions in each step as you arrive at insights, choices, and initial decisions. Plan to revisit your map at least every three months as you make progress. You may accelerate some plans, eliminate others, and discover new choices once you have greater awareness about the six areas. You may also create a more detailed map that you use to chart and check your progress every day, week, or month. Plan on an annual check-up to celebrate yourself and revisit some of your foundational decisions.

Step 1: Imagine the End of Your Story

Reflective Question

If you were at the end of your life story, looking back, what would make you feel that your life was well-lived?

Let's dive into how your values might inform every dimension of your journey.

Exploring Foundational Values

To help you uncover what's significant to you in terms of five important values (wisdom, power, unity, adventure, and contentment), circle one measure of the Likert scale (ranging from "Strongly Agree" to "Strongly Disagree") to indicate how much you resonate with each value.

WISDOM

"I believe that gaining knowledge and understanding is a lifelong pursuit, and I prioritize learning from both successes and failures."

STRONGLY AGREE   AGREE   NEUTRAL   DISAGREE   STRONGLY DISAGREE

POWER

"I value wielding influence and authority because they allow me to make meaningful decisions and positively impact those around me."

STRONGLY AGREE   AGREE   NEUTRAL   DISAGREE   STRONGLY DISAGREE

UNITY

"Building strong, supportive, and harmonious relationships is one of my core motivations in both personal and professional areas of my life."

STRONGLY AGREE   AGREE   NEUTRAL   DISAGREE   STRONGLY DISAGREE

ADVENTURE

"I seek new experiences, enjoy taking risks, and feel most fulfilled when I am exploring the unknown or challenging myself in unfamiliar situations."

STRONGLY AGREE   AGREE   NEUTRAL   DISAGREE   STRONGLY DISAGREE

CONTENTMENT

"I am motivated by a sense of inner peace and satisfaction, and I prioritize maintaining balance and tranquility in my life over constantly seeking new goals."

STRONGLY AGREE   AGREE   NEUTRAL   DISAGREE   STRONGLY DISAGREE

Reflection on Results

Once you complete the Likert scale for each of the five values, reflect on why certain values are the most significant to you.

Are there any values that surprised you as being more important than you initially thought?

What is the origin of your prizing the values in the statements you strongly agree with?

What life and work goals align with the values that you hold in highest regard?

How might you refocus your efforts in life—what changes could you make to bring more alignment between your actions and your core values?

Step 2: Planning Your Career and Professional Development

Reflective Questions

If you were to look back on your career after 20 years, what key moments or milestones would fill you with pride and satisfaction?

What compelling stories do you want to share about your career journey when you are reflecting 10 years from today?

What professional accomplishments or bold attempts will you be proud of when you look back in 5 years from today?

What career achievement do you want to celebrate at the end of this year? For example, securing a promotion, launching a business, pivoting careers, delivering keynote speeches, organizing a major industry event, making a significant contribution to your field's science or technology, or receiving a prestigious award.

Actions

With those professional or career milestones in mind, respond to the following.

Identify the skills, credentials, or experiences required to achieve your professional vision.

Research and list networking opportunities that could accelerate your growth (e.g., industry events, alumni gatherings, or mastermind groups).

Explore relevant workshops, seminars, or retreats that align with your career goals.

Create a timeline for acquiring necessary skills or credentials. (*Tip:* Be specific. What exactly do you need, and where will you obtain it? When will you conduct the research to find ideal solutions? When will you choose the right actions and schedule them on your calendar?)

Stay on Course—List Your Milestones

❑ Achieve   by

❑ Lead   by

❑ Launch   by

What other milestones align with your reflections and goals?

Pitfalls to Avoid

- ✗ Overcommitting to multiple paths without a clear focus or strategy
- ✗ Allowing fear of failure or "imposter syndrome" to hinder your career progression
- ✗ Neglecting to build a strong professional network or seek mentorship

Step 3: Financial Stability and Growth

Reflective Questions

1. Envision your ideal financial situation 20 years from now. What specific milestones or achievements will you have reached?

What level of financial freedom or security do you see for yourself and your family?

How will your lifestyle reflect your financial goals?

2. If you were looking back 10 years from today, what key financial decisions will you be proud to have made?

What investments or savings strategies will have paid off?

How will these choices have impacted both your short-term comfort and long-term financial growth?

3. Five years from now, what financial risks or opportunities will you be glad you seized?

What financial habits or strategies will you have implemented that set you up for success?

How will you have diversified or grown your income streams?

4. By the end of this year, what major financial goal do you want to celebrate achieving?

Whether it's reducing debt, increasing savings, or making a significant investment, how will accomplishing this goal make you feel?

How will this achievement set the foundation for your future financial growth?

Actions

1. Outline three financial plans, including strategies for savings, investments, and debt reduction:
   a. Short-term (1-3 years)
   b. Mid-term (4-7 years)
   c. Long-term (8+ years)
2. Schedule a consultation with a financial professional to ensure your plans align with your long-term goals.
3. Create a monthly budget that supports your financial goals while allowing for some flexibility and enjoyment.
4. Set up automatic transfers to savings and investment accounts to ensure consistent progress towards your goals.
5. Identify areas where you can increase your financial literacy (e.g., books, courses, workshops) and schedule time for this learning.

On-Course Milestones

Tip: Be specific. What exact steps will you take to reach each milestone? When will you review and adjust your financial strategies?

❑ Pay off

   by

❑ Achieve $ in retirement savings by

❑ Create an emergency fund covering   months of expenses

   by

❑ Increase net worth by   % within   years

Pitfalls to Avoid

✗ Neglecting long-term savings for short-term indulgences
✗ Incurring unnecessary debt without a clear repayment strategy
✗ Failing to diversify investments or relying too heavily on a single income stream
✗ Ignoring the impact of inflation on long-term financial planning

Step 4: Health and Well-being

What does it mean to feel truly mentally and emotionally fulfilled, in your ideal state of mind and body? What internal shifts do you need to make to reach those states? What obstacles do you need to release or overcome to give you the freedom to feel well?

Reflective Questions

1. What does "being in the best health of your life" mean to you, and how will achieving this change the way you experience the world, your relationships, and your daily life?

How will it feel to wake up each day knowing your body is strong, your mind is clear, and you're in harmony with yourself?

What would you be able to do physically and mentally that you can't do now, and how will those abilities open new doors for adventure, connection, and joy?

What experiences, achievements, or states of being are you longing for that improved health could bring within your reach?

2. How can you challenge yourself physically and mentally by selecting a sport, event, or adventure that pushes your limits and requires preparation?

What sport, fitness event (such as a marathon, triathlon, or hiking challenge), or adventurous vacation (such as a mountain trek, surfing retreat, or cycling tour) excites and motivates you?

What specific fitness, nutrition, or wellness plan would you need to create to prepare for this challenge?

How will accomplishing this challenge contribute to your overall health and sense of achievement?

3. Imagine you're living a life where you feel mentally sharp, emotionally balanced, and at peace every day—what does that look and feel like for you?

What thoughts and emotions fill your mind when you wake up and when you go to sleep?

How do you interact with challenges, and what practices will allow you to maintain this sense of clarity and calm even when life gets overwhelming?

What will you let go of—fears, beliefs, or patterns—that currently stand in the way of achieving this level of mental and emotional well-being?

Actions

1 Craft your personal definition of "best health" in writing, encompassing physical, mental, and emotional aspects.

2 Conduct a comprehensive health assessment as you feel is ideal. For example:
- ✓ Schedule a full physical check-up with your doctor.
- ✓ Complete a mental health self-assessment.
- ✓ Keep a mood and energy journal for two weeks.
- ✓ Track the hours and quality of your sleep to assess how well your support your mental and physical recovery requirements.

3 Research and select a challenging physical event or adventure.
- ✓ List potential options (e.g., marathon, mountain trek, triathlon).

- ✓ Evaluate each option based on your interests and current fitness level.
- ✓ Choose one event and register or set a date.

④ Create a holistic wellness plan:

    ✓ Design a workout routine (cardio, strength, flexibility).

    ✓ Develop a nutrition plan that supports your health goals.

    ✓ Establish a sleep hygiene routine.

    ✓ Incorporate stress-management techniques (e.g., meditation, yoga).

    ✓ Research and select a wellness coach or personal trainer.

    ✓ Join a fitness class or sports team.

    ✓ Find an accountability partner for your health journey.

⑤ Implement daily mindfulness practices.

    ✓ Choose a meditation app or guided practice.

    ✓ Set aside dedicated time each day for mindfulness.

    ✓ Keep a journal.

⑥ Identify and plan to address mental and emotional barriers.

    ✓ List some of your limiting beliefs.

    ✓ Create an action plan to gradually face and overcome each obstacle.

On-Course Milestones

Short-term (3-6 months)

❑ Complete initial health assessment and create wellness plan by

❑ Establish a consistent workout routine (e.g., 3-4 times per week)

by

❑ Meditate for   minutes daily for 30 consecutive days by

❑ Improve sleep quality (measure with sleep tracker or journal)

by

Mid-term (6-12 months)

❑ Achieve a specific fitness goal (e.g., run 5k in under 30 min.) by

❑ Reduce stress levels by   % (measured by self-assessment or

professional evaluation) by

❑ Complete a challenging physical event (e.g., half-marathon, mountain

trek) by

❑ Establish and maintain a balanced nutrition plan for 3 consecutive

months by

Long-term (1-3 years)

❑ Achieve and maintain a healthy body composition by

❑ Complete a major physical challenge (e.g., full marathon, triathlon)
by

❑ Develop and maintain a consistent work-life balance for 6 consecutive
months by

❑ Eliminate or significantly reduce a harmful habit (e.g., excessive alcohol
consumption, smoking) by

Ongoing

❑ Continuously educate yourself on health and wellness. (Read one
health-related book or attend one wellness seminar per quarter.)

Pitfalls to Avoid

✗ Pursuing unsustainable or extreme diet or exercise regimens
✗ Neglecting mental and emotional health while focusing solely on
physical fitness
✗ Comparing your progress to others instead of focusing on personal growth
✗ Ignoring the importance of rest and recovery in your wellness journey
✗ Failing to adjust your health goals as your life circumstances change

Step 5: Personal Development and Learning

Personal transformation can come from learning or acquiring new skills that might change your sense of limitations about your life experience, abilities, or options.

Reflective Questions

If you were to envision the most evolved, knowledgeable, and fulfilled version of yourself, what would you know, and how would you have transformed through learning and growth?

What areas of curiosity, creativity, or expertise light a fire inside you, pushing you toward mastery?

How would deepening your understanding in these areas change not just what you do, but who you become?

What knowledge or skills will help you not only achieve your goals, but also expand your sense of self and purpose?

Actions

Take this section incrementally—don't get overwhelmed. For example, you might do a little bit each week. Or, select just one action step that makes sense for you at this stage of your career. Then, put off the other steps for when you have more time or clarity. Making even a small amount of progress is great—don't think you need to do everything to make positive changes!

1 Conduct a personal skills audit.
- ✓ List your current skills and areas of expertise.
- ✓ Identify gaps between your current skills and those needed for your ideal self.

2 Create a personalized learning plan.
- ✓ Set specific learning goals for the next 3, 6, and 12 months.
- ✓ Research courses, workshops, or mentorship opportunities that align with your goals.
- ✓ Allocate a specific budget for personal development activities.

3 Establish a daily learning routine.
- ✓ Set aside 30-60 minutes each day for focused learning.
- ✓ Create a reading list of books that support your growth areas.
- ✓ Subscribe to relevant podcasts or online courses.

4 Seek out challenging experiences.
- ✓ Volunteer for projects outside your comfort zone at work or in your community.
- ✓ Attend conferences or workshops in fields that interest you.
- ✓ Join a local club or group related to a skill you want to develop.

5 Practice self-reflection.
- ✓ Start a journal to document your learning journey and insights.
- ✓ Schedule monthly self-assessment sessions to review progress and adjust goals.

On-Course Milestones

Short-term (3-6 months)

❑ Complete personal skills audit and create learning plan by

❑ Enroll in a course/workshop related to your primary growth area by

❑ Read   books on your chosen subjects by

❑ Maintain a daily learning routine for 30 consecutive days by

Mid-term (6-12 months)

❑ Achieve measurable improvement in

as evidenced by   by

❑ Present a lecture or workshop on a topic you've been studying by

❑ Complete a significant project that showcases your new skills by

❑ Mentor someone in an area where you've developed expertise by

Long-term (1-3 years)

❑ Obtain a relevant certification or degree in your chosen field by

❑ Publish an article or content demonstrating your expertise by

❑ Transition to a role/career aligned with your developed skills by

❑ Launch a business/side project leveraging your new knowledge by

Pitfalls to Avoid

- ✗ Spreading yourself too thin by pursuing too many learning goals simultaneously
- ✗ Neglecting to apply new knowledge in practical, real-world situations
- ✗ Allowing perfectionism to prevent you from taking action or sharing your work
- ✗ Focusing solely on professional skills at the expense of personal growth and well-being
- ✗ Failing to celebrate small wins and progress along your learning journey

Step 6: Relationships and Social Connections

Reflective Questions

What legacy do you want to leave for your family, friends, and community, and how will the way you nurture these relationships today shape that legacy?

How do you want people to feel after spending time with you, and what do you hope they remember most about their connection with you?

What kind of relationships will challenge you to grow while offering you the opportunity to help others flourish as well?

How will you ensure that the relationships you build contribute not only to your happiness but also to the broader well-being of your community?

How do you envision transforming your relationships with family, friends, and your community so they are more meaningful, joyful, and stable?

Actions

1. Conduct a relationship audit.
   - ✓ List your key relationships and assess their current state.
   - ✓ Identify areas for improvement or reconnection.
2. Create a relationship nurturing plan.
   - ✓ Set specific goals for strengthening important relationships.
   - ✓ Plan regular check-ins or quality time with loved ones.
   - ✓ Identify new social circles or communities to engage with.
3. Develop active listening and empathy skills.
   - ✓ Practice mindful listening in conversations.
   - ✓ Attend a workshop on emotional intelligence or communication skills.
4. Engage in community-building activities.
   - ✓ Volunteer for a local organization.
   - ✓ Join or start a community group aligned with your interests.
   - ✓ Organize neighborhood events or gatherings.
5. Practice celebration, gratitude, and appreciation.
   - ✓ Start a journal focusing on the positive aspects of your relationships.
   - ✓ Express appreciation to someone in your life each day.
6. Cultivate new relationships.
   - ✓ Attend networking events or join clubs related to your interests.
   - ✓ Use social apps or platforms to connect with like-minded individuals.
   - ✓ Initiate conversations with new people in your daily life.

On-Course Milestones

Short-term (3-6 months)

❑ Have meaningful, one-on-one conversations with   friends or family members by

❑ Join a new social group or community organization by

❑ Organize a gathering/event for friends/community members by

❑ Establish a weekly ritual for connecting with a loved one by

Mid-term (6-12 months)

❑ Deepen   existing relationships through regular quality time and shared experiences by

❑ Mend or improve a challenging relationship by

❑ Take on a leadership role in a community organization by

❑ Host a large gathering bringing together various social circles by

Long-term (1-3 years)

❑ Cultivate   new close friendships by

❑ Establish a mentoring relationship (as mentor or mentee) by

❑ Create lasting impact in your community through sustained involvement by

❑ Plan and execute a significant family or friend reunion by

Pitfalls to Avoid

- ✗ Neglecting existing relationships while pursuing new ones
- ✗ Allowing digital communication to replace meaningful in-person interactions
- ✗ Avoiding difficult conversations or conflict resolution in important relationships
- ✗ Overcommitting socially at the expense of personal well-being and self-care
- ✗ Maintaining toxic or one-sided relationships that drain your energy and positivity

Step 7: Purpose and Contribution

Reflective Questions

What unique gifts, experiences, or perspectives do you possess that the world needs, and how will you ensure that your life's work contributes to something larger than yourself?

In what ways do you feel called to serve others, whether through your profession, community, or personal passions?

How will you know that the work you've done and the impact you've had are aligned with your deepest values and the change you want to see in the world?

How do you envision the ripple effect of your contributions long after you're gone, and what steps can you take now to ensure those ripples are felt?

Actions

① Identify your core values and passions.
- ✓ Spend time reflecting on what matters to you and what drives you.
- ✓ List activities or causes that energize and inspire you.

② Research areas of need aligned with your interests.
- ✓ Explore local and global issues that resonate with you.
- ✓ Identify organizations or movements already working in these areas.

③ Develop a personal mission statement.
- ✓ Craft a clear, concise statement of your purpose and desired impact.
- ✓ Share your mission statement with trusted friends or mentors for feedback.

④ Create an action plan for your chosen purpose.
- ✓ Set specific, measurable goals for your contribution.
- ✓ Break down long-term objectives into actionable steps.

⑤ Build a support network.
- ✓ Identify potential mentors, collaborators, or supporters.
- ✓ Join or create a group of like-minded individuals working towards similar goals.

⑥ Integrate purpose into your daily life.
- ✓ Align your career or business with your mission where possible.
- ✓ Incorporate purposeful actions into your daily routine.

⑦ Develop skills needed for your purpose.
- ✓ Identify key skills required to make your desired impact.
- ✓ Create a learning plan to acquire or improve these skills.

On-Course Milestones

Short-term (3-6 months)

❑ Complete personal mission statement by

❑ Volunteer with   organizations aligned with your purpose by

❑ Attend   events/workshops related to your chosen cause by

❑ Initiate   conversations with potential mentors/collaborators by

Mid-term (6-12 months)

❑ Launch a personal project/initiative related to your purpose by

❑ Secure a role or position that aligns with your mission by

❑ Reach   people through your purpose-driven work by

❑ Raise $ or contribute   hours to your chosen cause by

Long-term (1-3 years)

❑ Create a sustainable program/organization furthering your mission by

❑ Mentor   individuals in your area of expertise or passion by

❑ Speak at a conference/event about your purpose-driven work by

❑ Achieve a measurable impact in your chosen field (e.g., policy change, lives improved) by

Pitfalls to Avoid

- ✘ Becoming overwhelmed by the scale of issues you want to address
- ✘ Neglecting self-care and personal well-being in pursuit of your purpose
- ✘ Allowing setbacks or slow progress to discourage you from your mission
- ✘ Focusing too narrowly on a single approach to achieving your purpose
- ✘ Losing sight of your original motivation and passion amid day-to-day tasks

Remember, your purpose may evolve over time. Regularly reassess your goals and impact. Be open to new ways of contributing to the world around you.

Final Step: Maintain Perspective

While each day may bring highs and lows, always keep the bigger picture in mind. Having clear goals and actions mapped out allows for resilience when faced with temporary setbacks. Regularly revisit your Life Journey Map to celebrate progress, adjust course as needed, and stay aligned with your evolving vision for a fulfilling life.

The Pierce Life Journey Map helps you reflect on your life goals in a structured way, breaking down your dreams and ambitions into actionable steps, and identifying potential challenges (and how to overcome them) along the way.

Live your life on course!

WHEN IT IS OBVIOUS THAT THE GOALS CANNOT BE REACHED,
DON'T ADJUST THE GOALS, ADJUST THE ACTION STEPS.

—CONFUCIUS

PART II
TRANSFORMING PRESSURE INTO POWER

Go confidently in the direction of your dreams.
Live the life you have imagined.
—Henry David Thoreau

MISERY, ENERGY, AND TIME

A personal reflection by
John Pierce

All the pressure you're feeling? It's a privilege. Let me say it again. All the pressure that you're feeling is truly a privilege. Why? Pressure produces extraordinary results. Pressure has a way of compressing energy, time, particles, and misery. This might be an incredible opportunity if you can find the strength to manage yourself through it.

If you can bear it, the force will work with you—almost through you—to get results that can't be found in the regular order and customary ways that comes "naturally." So really, if you can find a way to do what needs to be done, how could pressure be anything but a privilege? True, you might need to summon all your powers to wield the pressure as a tool and not be flattened by it or knocked down by it. If you can, you may find you have almost otherworldly finesse. Grace under pressure.

Now, not everyone has equal footing. Some people need more resources to deal with an increased load of stress and expectations. Help might come from a mentor, a sherpa, a sounding board, or a coach. Think about what you need and see if you can get access to it. That's part of learning how to manage pressure, and thinking of it as a privilege.

Disclaimer: Because I am a white guy in the financial services industry for over 30 years, I've got a very particular lens on pressure being a privilege. The reality struck me when I was working on my doctoral dissertation, which focused on coaching and mentoring for mid-career professionals. I never realized how my experience was, in so many ways, easier than others had it in the workplace.

When I say pressure is a privilege, I'm not referring to the pressure to overcome racial and gender bias in order to have a career or succeed. That realization was a major wake up call for me and one of my motivations for writing this book.

So, keep in mind when you have peers, colleagues, friends, or family members who are under pressure, it may be time to rethink what pressure might mean to them, and if you have it, use your privilege to help others.

6

HOW COULD PRESSURE BE A PRIVILEGE?

Diamonds. Penicillin. The civil rights movement. Olympic gold medals. Fusion energy. The perfect espresso.

What do these have in common? They're all products of extreme pressure.

In the natural world, pressure transforms ordinary carbon into extraordinary diamonds. In your career, it can do the same for you—if you understand how to harness it rather than be crushed by it.

Most people see pressure as the enemy. The deadlines that keep you up at night. The expectations that weigh on your shoulders. The competition breathing down your neck. The boss who's never satisfied. The family counting on you to provide.

I'm here to tell you what I've learned through three decades in financial services.

Pressure isn't your enemy—it's your advantage

When an ordinary chicken breast goes into a pressure cooker, it emerges transformed—tender, flavorful, infused with whatever spices surrounded it. When an ordinary career endures the right kind of pressure, the same transformation occurs—skills sharpen, decision-making improves, leadership emerges, creativity flourishes.

Pressure forces growth that comfort never could.

Think about it. When have you learned the most? When everything was easy, or when you were pushed to your limits? When have you been most creative? When you had unlimited time, or when the clock was ticking? When did you discover what you were capable of? When things were smooth sailing, or when you faced what seemed impossible?

The difference between those who thrive under pressure and those who crack isn't talent—it's perspective.

Some people see pressure as evidence that they're not good enough. Others see it as proof they're doing something that matters. Some feel pressure as a weight crushing them down. Others feel it as a force propelling them forward.

The pressure perspective: examples from real life

The difference between those who thrive under pressure and those who crack isn't talent—it's perspective.

Take Sarah and Michael, both project managers at a major tech company. Both were given the same impossible deadline: launch a new product feature in half the standard development time because a competitor was about to release something similar.

Sarah immediately went into crisis mode. She started working fourteen-hour days, micromanaging her team, and sending panicky late-night emails. When obstacles arose, she saw them as confirmation that the task was impossible. In fact, she was right—doing everything in the original specification wasn't possible—but she didn't stop to consider what could be cut out. Her dedication came from a good place but her anxiety was contagious, team morale plummeted, and mistakes multiplied. By the deadline, they had a buggy new feature and a burned-out team.

Michael approached the same pressure differently. In his first team meeting, he said, "This deadline means leadership trusts us to do something exceptional. They wouldn't have given us this challenge if they didn't believe we could handle it." He responded logically to the pressure but encouraging his team to eliminate non-essential features, streamline processes, and just focus on core functionality. When obstacles appeared, he'd repeat, "This is why they gave it to us—because we solve problems others can't." His team rallied, innovated, and delivered a streamlined but solid product on time.

Same pressure. Different perspectives. Different results.

Or consider what happens in presentations. I've watched promising executives crumble when asked to present to senior leadership. Jason, a brilliant analyst, would over-prepare for days, memorizing every word, and still freeze up when a C-suite executive asked an unexpected question. His perception? "They're testing me, and if I don't know the answer, they'll think I'm incompetent."

Meanwhile, his colleague Chloe approached the same presentations as opportunities. "If they're asking me questions, they're engaged with my ideas," she'd say. When she didn't know an answer, she'd respond, "That's an excellent question I haven't considered. I'll research that and follow up by end of day." Senior leaders began requesting Chloe for high-visibility projects not because she knew more than Jason, but because pressure brought out her best rather than his worst.

Even physical responses to pressure differ based on perspective. According to research from Harvard Business School, simply reframing anxiety as excitement—telling yourself "I'm excited" instead of "I'm nervous"— significantly improves performance under pressure.

I saw this play out dramatically during layoffs at a financial firm I worked with. Two division heads had to reduce their departments by 20%. The first saw it as a cruel burden, became depressed, avoided the office, and ultimately made arbitrary cuts that damaged team capabilities. The second reframed it: "This is painful but necessary. My job is to reshape this team to be as strong as possible—with fewer resources." By connecting with a sense of power from the pressure, the better leader could make strategic decisions, communicate transparently, and actually maintain department performance despite reduced headcount.

The pressure was identical. The perspective transformed the outcome.

I've witnessed this pattern repeatedly in acquisitions, market downturns, and regulatory changes. When pressure intensifies, some leaders become defensive, rigid, and focused on survival. Others become curious, adaptive, and focused on opportunity.

Your career will face constant pressure: impossible deadlines, difficult clients, intense competition, economic uncertainty. You cannot control these pressures. But you absolutely can control how you interpret them.

Is that aggressive deadline an unfair burden, or recognition of your capabilities? Is that difficult client a punishment, or a chance to demonstrate problem-solving or motivation to go after better clients? Is that new competitor a threat to your success, or motivation to innovate?

The choice—and it is a choice—will determine whether pressure diminishes or develops you.

The brutal truth? Pressure is a privilege that not everyone gets to experience.

Let me be clear: I'm not talking about the systemic pressures of inequality or hardship. Having inadequate resources, facing discrimination, or starting with disadvantages is not the kind of pressure I'm calling a privilege.

I'm talking about the pressure of high expectations. The pressure of responsibility. The pressure of opportunity. The pressure that comes when people believe you can deliver excellence.

During my career in financial services, I've operated in high-pressure environments that many never get the chance to experience. I've witnessed how privileges are unequally distributed—particularly among women and people of color who continue to be drastically underrepresented in our industry's leadership.

This hit home while I was researching my dissertation on coaching and mentoring mid-career professionals. The data showed that without proper support systems—mentors, coaches, advocates—pressure doesn't transform people; it breaks them.

That's why I'm passionate about equalizing access to the resources that help people turn pressure into power. Because when you have the right tools, pressure doesn't diminish you—it reveals what you're truly capable of.

If you're feeling the heat right now in your career, consider this reframe: You're not being punished. You're being forged. The pressure you feel isn't a sign that you're failing—it's a sign that you're playing at a level that matters.

The question isn't whether you'll face pressure. It's whether you'll use it as fuel or let it burn you out.

The privilege isn't in avoiding pressure—it's in having the resources, support, and mindset to transform it into your competitive advantage.

EXERCISE: THE PRESSURE PRIVILEGE INVENTORY

1. List three current sources of pressure in your professional life
2. For each, identify what this pressure is trying to create in you (e.g., better time management, clearer communication, strategic thinking)
3. Rate how well-resourced you are to handle each pressure (1-10)
4. For your lowest-rated pressure, identify one resource you could add (mentor, skill, tool, boundary) to transform it from crushing to catalyzing

QUESTION TO REFLECT ON

When was the last time pressure pushed you to achieve something you didn't think was possible? What resources helped you succeed?

FIRST STEP

Identify the single greatest pressure you're currently facing. Write down three ways this pressure, if channeled correctly, could actually accelerate your growth or create an opportunity. Choose one of these potential benefits and post it where you'll see it daily as a reminder of pressure's transformative power.

FIRST SAY TO YOURSELF WHAT YOU WOULD BE;
AND THEN DO WHAT YOU HAVE TO DO.

—EPICTETUS

7

LOOKING FOR ADVICE IN
ALL THE WRONG PLACES

Let me tell you something most people never figure out: the advice that feels good rarely makes you stronger. It might stroke your ego. It might calm you down. It might make you optimistic. But advice that doesn't make you think most likely is shortchanging your ability to grow and meet your goals.

You know the routine. You hit a career obstacle—a difficult boss, a failed project, a peer who's advancing faster—and you seek comfort. You call your friend who always takes your side. You consult your spouse who loves you unconditionally. You vent to colleagues who share your frustrations.

What do they tell you? Exactly what you want to hear.

"Your boss is unreasonable." "That project was impossible from the start." "That promotion should have been yours."

This validation feels like oxygen when you're drowning in self-doubt. But here's the brutal truth:

The complaint trap

Let's talk about your complaining habit. Yes, you have one. We all do.

Complaining feels productive. It feels like you're addressing the problem by articulating it. It feels like you're building alliances when others nod in agreement. It feels like you're processing emotions when you vent your frustrations.

You're doing none of those things.

What you're actually doing is rehearsing failure. Every time you recount how you were wronged, overlooked, or undervalued; you're strengthening neural pathways that keep you stuck in victim mode. You're teaching your brain that circumstances control your destiny rather than your responses to them.

The most successful people I've worked with aren't complaint-free—they just direct their complaints differently. Instead of saying "My boss doesn't appreciate me," they ask "What am I missing about what my boss values?" Instead of "This client is impossible," they wonder "What approach haven't I tried yet?"

This isn't semantics. It's the difference between pressure crushing you and pressure propelling you. It's accepting the reality that some people are problematic. Some people make things difficult. That a significant amount of life is unfair. That doesn't mean you can't prevail—it just means you must find a way to succeed that isn't obvious.

Next time you feel the urge to complain, try this: set a timer for two minutes. Complain with full intensity until the timer sounds. Then stop. Completely. Turn your attention to what you can control, alternative ways to solve the problem, and what you can influence. That way, you get the relief of venting without the trap of dwelling.

Managing well-meaning interference

Here's another challenge: what to say when friends, family, and coworkers want to comment on your obvious frustration, anger, or distress.

These conversations often sound like: "You seem stressed. Is everything okay?" "If I were you, I wouldn't stand for that treatment." "You should just tell your boss exactly how you feel."

These people care about you. Their intentions are good. Their advice is terrible.

How do you handle this without damaging relationships? With prepared responses that honor their concern while protecting your growth:

To friends and family: "I appreciate your concern, and I'm working through this systematically. What would help most is if you could just listen without trying to solve it for now. I'm building my resilience muscles."

To colleagues: "Thanks for checking in. I'm actually using this situation as an opportunity to develop new skills. If you've faced something similar, I'd be interested in hearing what worked for you professionally."

To your boss: "I've been reflecting on your feedback and want to make sure I'm addressing the core issues. Could we schedule 15 minutes to clarify expectations so I can focus my development efforts?"

The key is redirecting well-meaning interference toward productive support. You're not shutting them down—you're channeling their desire to help in ways that actually help.

Every time you successfully navigate these conversations without sliding into complaint mode, you're transforming social pressure into interpersonal power.

The high cost of poor advice

A heart surgeon doesn't remove cataracts. The dentist doesn't set broken bones. And your well-meaning friend can't coach you to success in the corporate arena—no matter how much they care. Much less those odd situations where someone close to you revels in your difficulties, often without your suspecting that.

Remind yourself that asking the wrong people for help is making you weaker, not stronger.

When do you actually need a qualified coach? Earlier than you think.

When the first hint of conflict with your boss emerges—not after you've exchanged heated words. When you begin feeling overwhelmed—not after you've missed three deadlines. When performance feedback highlights weaknesses—not after you've been put on a performance improvement plan.

But especially when you're labeled "high potential"—because that's when the stakes get highest and the blind spots get costliest.

Being smart can make you weak

Here's the paradox I've seen repeatedly in my three decades in financial services: the smarter you are, the more you need coaching. Your cognitive brilliance—the very thing that got you noticed—becomes your greatest vulnerability.

Why? Because intelligence without awareness is like horsepower without steering.

I learned this lesson the hard way in a position I recently held. After years of success leading my division, I hit a rough patch. New private equity ownership, compensation challenges for recruiting, a transition year by any measure. I focused intensely on rebuilding for the future, confident that my track record would buy me time.

I was wrong. Catastrophically wrong.

While I calculated future returns, I missed the political calculus happening around me. I didn't see the non-verbal cues from leadership. I failed to recognize that my position had become a prize for others. I was so focused on the road ahead that I had a blind spot where other executives were keen on self-preservation.

My job was eliminated. My future with the company erased.

Had I employed even basic spatial intelligence—the ability F1 racing drivers use to sense where every car is on the track while driving 220 mph—I could have navigated differently. I'd have seen the threats emerging and adjusted my strategy accordingly.

Read the room

This isn't unique to my situation. Most career-ending mistakes begin with perception gaps, not competence gaps. The director who can't read the room. The VP who can't regulate their emotions under pressure. The manager who can't see how their communication style alienates others. The leader who has a problem with alcohol or other substances.

These blind spots won't heal themselves with time—they'll compound. Practice doesn't make perfect; practice makes permanent. If you're practicing dysfunction, you're perfecting dysfunction.

Think of it this way: emotional intelligence is to corporate success what endurance is to marathon runners. When you hit mile 18, your body depleted and muscles burning, it's not physical training alone that carries you forward—it's mental resilience. The ability to feel discomfort without being derailed by it.

The corporate equivalent happens daily. Facing criticism without becoming defensive. Navigating uncertainty without showing anxiety. Processing disappointment without losing focus. Dealing with difficult personalities without becoming one yourself.

These are learnable skills—but not through trial and error, and certainly not through well-meaning but misguided advice from those who care about your feelings more than your growth.

Transforming pressure into power requires someone who sees what you can't see, asks what others won't ask, and tells you what you might not want to hear—but absolutely need to know.

EXERCISE: THE COMPLAINT CONVERSION

1. Keep a complaint log for three days, noting every time you complain and to whom
2. Next to each complaint, write what you wanted from that interaction (sympathy, solutions, connection)
3. Rewrite each complaint as a power statement: "I don't know how to handle this" becomes "I need to develop a strategy for this"
4. Practice your power statements in the mirror, saying them aloud until they feel natural

QUESTION TO REFLECT ON

When was the last time you felt better—truly better, not just temporarily relieved—after complaining about a work situation?

FIRST STEP

Create three response templates for redirecting well-meaning advice from family, friends, and colleagues. Keep them in your phone's notes app so you're prepared when these conversations arise, rather than falling back into complaint mode by default.

WHEN CORPORATE LIFE LIMITS YOU, RUN

A personal reflection by

Matt Livingstone

BRAND MARKETER AND LONG (LONG) DISTANCE RUNNER

Find a way to get control over your life and time.

When work doesn't actualize all your drive, find your own way to channel it.

When I graduated from Villanova University with multiple degrees and no clear direction, I felt lost, like my life was happening to me rather than being shaped by me. In an attempt to take back control, I laced up my sneakers and hit the road. In the early days I wasn't fast, and I didn't go far, but for the first time in a long time, I was the one deciding where I was going.

Next thing I knew, someone mentioned a ten-mile race. At the time, running even a single mile felt like a struggle, and the idea of ten seemed impossible. But with dedication and perseverance, I made it to the finish line. And with that came the question: What's next? Turns out when you run, there's lots of places you can go to do it—and I did. I ran my first 100-mile race and went on to race on the Appalachian Trail, Mount Rushmore, and most recently, Mt. Blanc.

The Endurance Mindset: Turning goals into achievements

Acronyms are ridiculous (see CHUNK below) but so is running 110 miles with over 33,000 ft of elevation gain as I found out while running the Ultra-Trail du Mont-Blanc in 2024. I've been training and racing endurance events for over 12 years, highlighted by multiple top 10 and sub-24hr 100-mile finishes, running

216 miles around Lake Tahoe, and enough treadmill miles to make a hamster jealous. When it comes to chasing seemingly impossible goals, I've found that this simple acronym keeps me focused and moving forward.

Chase your goals: Set your sights on what you want and go get it. Don't just hope for progress; actively chase it. Every day, every effort brings you closer to what might seem impossible. Embrace the challenge, because the pursuit of these "big hairy audacious goals" is what drives real growth. The bigger and stupider the goal, the greater the reward.

Hurt: It's ok! Many of us work desk jobs, risking cramped fingers over any real source of discomfort. But it is ok to feel some pain. Recognize it. Lean into it. This pain is temporary, but the growth you gain from pushing through it is lasting. Every ache is a reminder that you're challenging yourself, expanding your limits, and moving toward something better.

Understand: Know thyself. It's not just about enduring physical discomfort; true growth begins with recognizing your mental boundaries. Understand where you're comfortable and make the choice to push past those limits. Comfort is safe, but it quickly becomes a trap that prevents true progress. When your success depends on endurance, mental complacency is just as dangerous as physical fatigue.

Never stop: Every step gets you closer to your goal. Your mind will scream at you to quit, sending countless reasons to stop, but that's where the real challenge lies. It is a long way between your brain and your legs, disrupt the connection between doubt and action and keep going.

Keep calm: And carry on (not just a cliché poster). Adversity breeds resilience and both are inevitable in ultra races, as in life. Unexpected challenges will arise, testing your patience, resolve, and focus. But what truly defines you is how you respond. Take control of what you can and let go of what you can't.

That's CHUNK: The most important aspects of the endurance mindset.

C—Chase your goals.

H—Hurt and get through it.

U—Understand yourself.

N—Never stop.

K—Keep calm and carry on.

Don't view an entire race or challenge as one massive, overwhelming task. Break it down into manageable pieces. A journey can seem daunting, but a step is achievable. By 'chunking' your effort, you can transform the impossible into the possible. One step, repeated again and again (and again), gets you to the where you want to go.

Today, I work a sedentary job where my biggest physical risk is carpal tunnel, but running remains my way to push my limits, feel alive and reclaim control in a world that constantly tries to take it away.

Here's the truth. Your career cannot be everything in your life. Find something outside of work that you truly own—where you make the decisions, where you test yourself, and where you are judge of a good day's work.

ABOUT MATT LIVINGSTONE

Matt Livingstone is a much-lauded marketer and brand strategist providing creative leadership at a major advertising agency. He and his teams have produced award-winning campaigns for some of the largest national and global brands. His business career achievements are rivaled by the accomplishments he has racked up during his 12-year endurance running career, with multiple top 10 and sub-24 hour 100-mile finishes.

IT IS NOT THAT WE HAVE A SHORT TIME TO LIVE,
BUT THAT WE WASTE A LOT OF IT.

—SENECA

8

WHEN THE RUNWAY SEEMS TOO SHORT, BUILD WINGS ON THE WAY DOWN

L et's talk about the cramping pain in your stomach when you're facing a deadline that you're not ready for. That blinding headache the moment your boss gives you a project with half the time it deserves. Your dry mouth when you realize you need to deliver results now, despite having incomplete information, insufficient resources, or inadequate preparation.

Most people respond to short runways in predictable ways: they feel sick, panic, they cut corners, or they lower expectations. "This isn't enough time," they say. "No one could possibly succeed under these conditions." Then they either choke and come up with nothing, rush through sloppy work, or make excuses about what they can't do before they've even tried.

But here's what the most successful people in any organization understand: the ability to perform under awful constraints or with diminished capacity isn't just a handy career skill—it's the foundation of unshakable confidence. You might call it determined or even delusional optimism, but the response you have to this type of pressure changes how people see you. That changes the opportunities you're awarded.

Pilots determined to make it back to base after their planes have been all but shot down during a battle in the air, call it flying home on a wing and a prayer.

I saw this determination firsthand with Rachel, a financial analyst at a global investment firm. Three days before a critical client presentation, her director fell seriously ill. Despite being the most junior team member, Rachel was tapped to deliver the analysis to the client's executive board—work she had contributed to but hadn't led much less understood in total, for a client relationship worth millions.

"I thought my career was over before it really began," she told me later. But instead of focusing on her lack of preparation time, Rachel made a critical decision. "If I can't extend the runway, I need to build a different set of wings."

She spent the first four hours identifying exactly what the client needed versus what her team had planned to present. She reached out to senior colleagues in different departments who had similar cases and borrowed their frameworks and graphics. Rather than attempting to master every technical detail, she focused on the strategic implications the client cared about most.

When presentation day came, Rachel opened with candor: "I'm not going to pretend to have all the answers today. What I do have is the most critical insights you need for your decision, and the commitment to get you anything else within 24 hours." That authentic portrayal of the situation actually built more trust than a polished performance would have, and resulted in a three-year contract renewal.

The difference between those who build wings on the way down and those who crash isn't resources or even talent—it's their response to constraints.

Wing-builders ask different questions

Instead of "Why me?" they ask, "What's possible?" Instead of "Who's to blame?" they ask, "Who can help?" Instead of "How did we get here?" they ask, "Where do we go from here?"

This mindset shift creates what psychologists call "challenge stress" rather than "threat stress." The physiological symptoms might feel similar—racing heart, heightened awareness—but challenge stress enhances performance while threat stress destroys it.

Stress does not equal distress if you recognize there's always opportunity, even if it looks very different than you expected or wished.

Here's how to shift from threat to challenge when your runway looks impossibly short:

First, **accept reality** exactly as it is. Not as you wish it were. Not as it "should" be. The runway is short. Period. Wasting energy on resistance only burns the little fuel you have left.

Second, **redefine success**. Perfect is rarely possible with tight constraints, but excellence still is. What's the 20% of work that will deliver 80% of the value? What's genuinely essential versus what's merely preferable? Your definition of success must align with what's actually possible.

Third, **leverage what you already have**. When there's no time to build from scratch, what existing assets, relationships, or knowledge can you repurpose? Who in your network has faced similar challenges? What past experiences, even in different contexts, might provide insights?

Fourth, **create micro-milestones**. When the finish line seems impossibly distant, establish smaller targets along the way. Each small win builds momentum and confidence for the next challenge. Think of lifting weights. You can boost your strength just by counting your reps and saying, "just three more to go! Three, two, one. Done!"

Fifth and finally, **maintain perspective**. Most short runways aren't actually life-or-death situations, despite how they feel in the moment. Your career won't end with one missed deadline when the conditions changed so close to a due date. Your worth isn't determined by perfect execution under imperfect conditions.

The confidence that comes from navigating short runways isn't about always sticking the landing. It's about knowing that regardless of how things turn out, you can respond with creativity, adaptability, and resilience.

Remember: Everyone faces short runways. Everyone feels unprepared sometimes but that doesn't have to shake your confidence. The difference is that some people let circumstances define their capabilities, while others let constraints reveal capabilities they didn't know they had.

EXERCISE: THE CONSTRAINT REFRAME

1. Identify a current challenge where you feel you don't have adequate time, information, or resources.
2. List three specific constraints that feel most limiting.
3. For each constraint, write one way it might actually serve as an advantage or catalyst for innovation.
4. Identify one "wing" you can build today—a small, immediate action or alternative approach that moves you forward despite limitations.
5. Consider sharing your approach with a mentor or soundboard for feedback or tweaks.

QUESTION TO REFLECT ON

When has a constraint in your career actually led to a better outcome than if you'd had unlimited resources or time?

FIRST STEP

Choose one upcoming project and deliberately build in a constraint—less time, fewer resources, or limited scope. Use it as practice for building your "wing-building" muscles in a controlled environment before you need them in a true free-fall situation.

A PERFECTLY HORRIBLE EXPERIENCE

A personal reflection by

John Pierce

Believe you can and you're halfway there.
—Theodore Roosevelt

lpe d'Huez is the most famous bike route in the Tour de France. I made the mistake of taking my family there because I saw they were holding part of a triathlon on the site, and figured I could use it as a family vacation while I also snuck in some exercise. So, I took the family and we popped into Paris, went on to Versailles, and then rode the train to Alpe d'Huez. We were in a bus going up the hill, and I could read on the faces of my family something like, "We're going to fall off this cliff, and how in the world is Dad going to ride up this hill?"

A few days later, I lined up with the competition as we started off with a small swim of about a mile. I had brought my wetsuit, a sleeveless wetsuit because I don't like long sleeves. It feels too constrained. That was a mistake. The water was 51 degrees, and as I was shivering, standing on a rock at the back, I'm like, "I'm not going to go in the water until I have to."

Like all bad things, eventually the time came and I hopped in the water, literally thinking I was going to get hypothermia. I'm swimming and some guy who doesn't know how to swim or wasn't paying attention was literally going 180 degrees in the wrong direction. He clocked me in the head and I sunk under the water. I'm like, "Wow, this is not how I want to start off the swim."

Finally, I emerged from the swim and jumped on my bike for maybe 20 miles until we got to the hill. So, first freezing cold water. Then, I'm sweating on my bike as I start going up the 21 switchbacks and think, "Wow, what did I get myself into?"

A few days earlier, I'd gone *down* about 10 of the switchbacks just to get a sense of it. At the time I thought, "Okay, this is okay." However, once you are going *up* those switchbacks, it is crazy. Literally the most difficult thing I've done on a bike. Totally unprepared in my training. Certainly, there was no hill training in South Jersey. So, I mentally told myself, "Okay, every time you get to a switchback, it feels like you're going faster. You just have to mentally grind through it. And then you get to the top of the hill."

At this point, I've been freezing in the water, sweating getting to the hill, feeling massive back pain up the hill, and suddenly I'm on a five-mile run and it's snowing on me. It was like, "Wow, I have all the seasons in one short race. Not at all what was in the brochure."

So, my first message to you is when you get in over your head, breathe. Whether it's at work, whether it's at an event, whether it's on a date, or whenever you realize things aren't going right, just breathe.

Secondly, finish. I enter races knowing that I am not going to win: not overall, not in my age group, not in any category that anyone else cares about. I've got one objective: finish.

When you're at work in over your head or you are faced with a challenge that just seems unbelievably difficult and there's no way you can do it: you can. Admit that it's perfectly awful. Breathe. And more importantly, just finish. That's the job. Just finish.

9

THE CONFIDENCE PARADOX: ADMITTING YOU DON'T KNOW MAKES YOU UNSTOPPABLE

Remember that guy in class who always raised his hand. He knew every answer and wanted everyone to know he did. He dominated class discussions. He was the most obnoxious and least liked person in the room. If knowledge was power, that guy would have been the big man on campus. He wasn't. No one likes a know-it-all who makes sure you know he is.

When I started in financial services, there was a manager named Richard who intimidated everyone. He'd built his reputation on being the smartest person in the room—the one with answers to every question, solutions to every problem, insights into every market movement. He knew the right people in the right places. He seemed to know it all and have it all. Maybe work wasn't like school, I thought.

In fact, when we saw him in meetings, we all wanted to be like Richard. We'd stay up late memorizing data, rehearsing responses to potential questions, and trying to build an arsenal of answers to protect ourselves against looking uninformed. The fear of looking stupid is a pretty good motivator. In fact, I once watched a colleague give a completely fabricated answer rather than admit uncertainty when Richard asked about an obscure regulatory change.

Three years later, Richard was fired. He couldn't keep up his perfect record. Knowledge gets old. Being Mr. Perfect or The Genius is a hard title to earn every day. Somewhere along his prestigious education and career journey,

Richard lost the ability to say, "I'm not sure, let me research that and get back to you." His unwillingness to acknowledge gaps in his knowledge led to a series of increasingly costly mistakes. The "always-have-an-answer" approach that had propelled his early career ultimately destroyed it.

Here's the paradox that Richard never understood: **True confidence isn't demonstrated by having all the answers all the time.** Confidence is communicated by being secure enough to admit when you don't.

This isn't just philosophical wisdom—it's practical career advice. In a rapidly changing business landscape, pretending to know everything isn't just risky; it's impossible. The half-life of professional knowledge is shrinking. What you learned in your MBA program three years ago is likely outdated. The technical certification you completed last year might be rendered obsolete by next quarter's innovation. Frankly, if you got news ten minutes ago, the situation may have already changed by the time you're talking about it.

The most respected leaders I've worked with don't hide behind a facade of omniscience. They practice what I call "strategic vulnerability"—the deliberate acknowledgment of limitations, deployed at the right time and in the right way.

Consider Pam, who took over a struggling division at a major consumer goods company. In her first leadership meeting, instead of pretending to have all the solutions, she said: "I have strong hypotheses about what's not working, but I need your expertise to test them. I don't yet understand all the operational constraints we're facing." Within six months, her division had reversed its decline, not because Pam knew everything, but because she created an environment where others were willing to dig in and contribute their knowledge.

Acknowledging gaps creates certainty about your character

The psychology here is fascinating. When you pretend to know everything, you create distance. People see you as either arrogant (if they believe you) or dishonest (if they don't). But when you thoughtfully acknowledge gaps in your knowledge, you create connection. You signal that you value truth over ego, learning over appearing learned.

But—and this is crucial—there's an art to effective "I don't know" statements. Blurting out "I have no idea" in every situation isn't confidence; it's abdication. Strategic vulnerability requires nuance.

Here's how to master the confidence paradox:

First, **separate facts from opinions**. "I don't know the Q3 revenue figures off the top of my head" is a straightforward admission about retrievable information. "I don't know if this strategy will work, so I want to discuss the downsides and alternatives that we can be ready to deploy" is more complex. It's an acknowledgment of future uncertainty that everyone shares, even if they won't admit it.

Second, **pair admission with action**. "I don't know, but I'll find out by working the numbers. I can have the answer tomorrow at 10 AM if this can wait until then" demonstrates both honesty and agency. "I don't know yet, but here's my approach to figuring it out" shows both humility and problem-solving capacity.

Third, **be selective**. Constantly saying "I don't know" about core job functions will undermine confidence in your competence. The sweet spot is acknowledging gaps in areas adjacent to your expertise—this signals both self-awareness and a growth mindset.

Fourth, **watch your body language and tone**. Delivering "I don't know" with eye contact, steady voice, and upright posture communicates security in your professional identity. Mumbling it while looking at the floor signals insecurity.

Fifth and finally, **recognize when others are practicing false confidence**. When someone gives a vague, jargon-filled answer, you might ask specific follow-up questions if you really need the information. When they make dubious claims, request to see how they came upon those conclusions, if you plan to work with them. You never want to embarrass anyone; you just want to protect yourself.

The ultimate expression of the confidence paradox is found in experts who have reached the pinnacle of their fields. They freely acknowledge the boundaries of their knowledge precisely because they're so secure in what they do know. They've moved beyond the beginner's need to appear infallible, which is a sure sign of insecurity.

That's your goal: not to need to know everything, but to be unshakable in your confidence that you can learn anything that matters.

EXERCISE: THE KNOWLEDGE AUDIT

1. List three topics in your field where you feel compelled to have all the answers
2. For each, write the real consequences of admitting you don't know everything
3. Draft a "strategic vulnerability" statement you could use when these topics arise
4. Identify one person whose expertise could help fill these knowledge gaps

QUESTION TO REFLECT ON

When did pretending to know something ultimately
cost you more than admitting you didn't?

FIRST STEP

In your next meeting, identify one appropriate opportunity to practice strategic vulnerability. Afterward, note how others responded and how it affected the quality of discussion and decision-making.

WITH REALIZATION OF ONE'S OWN POTENTIAL AND SELF-CONFIDENCE
IN ONE'S ABILITY, ONE CAN BUILD A BETTER WORLD.

—DALAI LAMA

LEARNING TO SAY OUCH WHEN YOUR PAIN IS REAL BUT UNSEEN

A personal reflection by

Jane Kim, M.D., EdD

EMERGENCY ROOM PHYSICIAN

What to do when brilliance + willpower = burnout

When the going gets rough, consider re-educating yourself

It's four in the morning in a pediatric emergency room in Central Brooklyn, New York. The final patient has been sent home and there are no more patients to be seen in the waiting room. I turn to my senior resident and ask, "So, what are you going to be now that you are all grown up?" Immediately, our pediatric emergency room is transformed into a confessional. I ask them several questions to guide them through their thinking and help them uncover their future direction. But somewhere along the talk, the tables get turned and, as always, I end up getting asked the same question, "Why did you decide to get a doctorate in education while working as a full-time emergency medicine doctor?"

My response and their reaction are also always the same.

I answer, "Because I was burnt out."

"Huh?" they respond with their head cocked to the side.

It doesn't make sense on the surface. But it makes perfect sense to get a second doctorate when you are experiencing burnout, at least it did for me.

Higher education has been my safe space. School is where I thrived. I've been on an elite educational superhighway all my formative years: gifted class elementary school, gifted class junior high school, specialized high school, top ten private university, graduate school, medical school, and residency in emergency medicine. I was bred to be an academic athlete. But in 2012, the superhighway ended abruptly with the end of my residency training and the beginning of my life as an attending emergency medicine physician.

Exiting a lifetime of education and training, then entering "real life" was an abrupt change I was unprepared to master when it happened.

True, I was all grown up. I became the doctor that I wanted to be. But I was told, and I believed at that time, that I needed to be *more* than just an emergency medicine physician. More. What was that "more" supposed to be?

Apparently, I required more than my job as a physician. I should add on a non-clinical role to "find my niche in medicine." If that were true, education was a logical fit. My mother was a math teacher, and my father was an English teacher back in Korea. I had helped run and create the curriculum for a medical student wilderness medicine course when I was a resident. So, medical student education seemed like the right niche for this additional responsibility, and I was encouraged by my mentors within the department who had known me since I was a first-year medical student. I believed that they had my best interest at heart. I believed that I was making the right decision for myself and my career, even though I didn't spend one second asking myself this question directly.

I consulted everyone but myself.

I dove headfirst into education as my non-clinical area of work. I started with medical student education and then moved on to healthcare simulation education. Simulation was the perfect blend of healthcare, education, and technology.

Two years after I became an attending physician, right out of residency training, I was named the director of the division of healthcare simulation for the Department of Emergency Medicine and the medical director of the simulation center for the entire medical university. Creating a curriculum and running simulation activities for medical students, residents, and attending physicians was easy.

The administrative role of being a director and medical director was difficult.

Medical training teaches you to be a good doctor, but it doesn't teach you to be a good teacher or leader. Medical school didn't teach me much outside of medicine.

I had all the ambition and drive in the world with no skill to make it happen. I felt confident about my skills as a teacher, but I was a terrible young leader.

I didn't acquire and didn't know how to acquire any resources to support myself or my team. We were constantly doing work without a budget or compensation. I was told that this was normal. "You have to pay into the system before you can reap the rewards", said my mentor. He called this "bodega mentality". A bodega is what New Yorkers call a corner deli with a cat that is open 24/7 and sells everything from prepared food, snacks, sodas, groceries, and household goods.

But I didn't want to work in a bodega. I became a doctor, not a Korean deli owner-operator. Somehow, I had bought into a system that wouldn't compensate me or support me and yet demanded everything I had.

I thought my academic achievements and smarts would help me play the political game. However, I didn't know how the game was even played.

No one stopped my blind ambition. I thought I could just brute force my way forward. If things were difficult, I would just work harder. But success only led to a vicious cycle of more work without resources because people thought our labor and services were free.

My team and I were victims of our success and a young naïve director. More work led to more despair. I was exhausted. I felt taken advantage of and underappreciated. I would ask, "Is this how medicine is?" I felt myself distancing myself not only from my non-clinical work within education but also from my clinical work.

Not even 5 years into my attending life, I wanted to leave medicine.

I wanted to be a better learning leader. I consider that this was a "me" problem that I could solve. I thought that I didn't have the right skills or knowledge. So, I decided to get a doctorate in education. I learned the language and framework for creating effective and evidence-based learning activities. I picked up the basic business skills to set up an operational learning organization that could be technologically innovative and revenue-generating. But the greatest skill that I gained was learning about myself.

I'd heard of burnout before starting my doctoral studies. I knew the statistic that four hundred physicians commit suicide a year. I sat through endless talks that touted the benefits of working out, sleeping more, and yoga. But I didn't know or think that I was burnt out.

Physicians aren't a very introspective bunch nor are Koreans as a group. So, it's a double whammy of mental health ignorance for me. My fellow doctoral students were learning leaders from diverse industries and in different stages of their careers. They listened, guided, and coached me to look at myself and evaluate what was going on in my work life.

My exhaustion, my feeling of being an ineffective leader, and my desire to leave medicine altogether were all clear symptoms of burnout. I hated to admit it.

My doctoral dissertation was on the topic of physician burnout versus well-being within the emergency room. It was a selfish way for me to learn how I ended up being burned out. The findings of my dissertation pointed to a theory that a physician who is "compassionate" and goes beyond the "knowledge" work and medical treatment of a patient ends up at a higher risk of experiencing burnout. Compassion is a double-edged sword: it's great for patient care but bad for physician care. My study did not propose a solution, it only illustrated another possible cause. The "cure" for physician burnout is not to stop being a compassionate physician.

After receiving my doctorate in education, though I didn't have all the answers, I felt better than when I started. Here are my gains.

1. I became aware of my feelings and practices at work.
2. I was able to directly ask myself questions about what I wanted to do next.
3. I no longer prioritized other's desires and suggestions over my needs and well-being.
4. I forced myself to do, at times difficult, self-work. Even now, asking myself questions and looking at myself is still uncomfortable.

Now as a postdoc doc, I asked myself, "What do I want to be when I grow up?" I want to help people, especially young emergency medicine physicians, navigate their professional transitions. I don't want them to succumb to another's vision for them. I want them to courageously craft their own story. Hopefully, this ability to do the self-work and live out their own journey will prevent some compassionate physicians from burning out and leaving the field of medicine.

I look forward to the day we have the "problem" of having too many compassionate doctors in healthcare who can also prioritize their own well-being.

ABOUT JANE KIM

Dr. Jane Kim is an emergency medicine attending physician in Brooklyn, New York, and previously worked as a leader in healthcare simulation. She enjoys hiking with her dog Oreo, snowboarding, and singing karaoke.

10

CONFIDENCE ISN'T BUILT IN THE SPOTLIGHT, BUT IN THE SHADOWS

The standing ovation. The promotion announcement. The awards ceremony. The successful product launch. These are the moments we associate with confidence—the public victories that seem to define successful careers.

But this perspective gets it exactly backward.

True confidence isn't built in the spotlight. It's forged in the shadows—in the quiet, unglamorous moments that no one sees or celebrates. It's developed through the daily disciplines, the private struggles, and the relentless preparation that happen long before any public recognition.

I learned this lesson from an unexpected source: Elaine, the seemingly "overnight success" who took over the marketing department at my previous firm. To outsiders, she appeared to have an almost supernatural confidence, presenting bold strategies to skeptical executives, navigating office politics with ease, and delivering results that garnered industry attention.

What most people never saw: Elaine waking up at 4:30 AM to research industry trends before her children stirred. The weekends spent testing different presentation approaches with a speaking coach. The meticulous preparation for every meeting, including researching the background and priorities of each attendee. The detailed post-mortem she conducted after every project, analyzing what worked and what didn't.

Her public success wasn't the source of her confidence—it was the result of it. The confidence had already been built, hour by hour, in the shadows.

Here's the challenging truth: If you're waiting for external validation to feel confident, you'll always be at the mercy of forces you can't control. Markets shift. Bosses change. Recognition gets delayed, misdirected, or stolen. The spotlight is fickle.

What remains constant is your ability to build what I call your "confidence infrastructure"—the internal foundation that supports you regardless of external circumstances.

This infrastructure has three essential components:

First, **deliberate practice**. Not just putting in hours, but intentionally focusing on your weaknesses, seeking feedback, and incrementally expanding your capabilities. When you know you've prepared more thoroughly than required, you develop the quiet certainty that you can handle whatever challenges emerge.

Consider the distinction between two ways to prepare for a presentation. One person reviews their slides the night before, hoping everything goes well. Another person practices delivering the key points while intentionally introducing distractions like washing the dishes or having a podcast in the background, prepares responses to potential objections and says them aloud, and then records themselves to identify unattractive habits like swaying or touching their face. The first approach leaves confidence to chance; the second builds it systematically.

Second, **reflection rituals**. Confidence gained simply erodes when we don't process our experiences. Create regular intervals—daily, weekly, monthly—to examine what's working, what isn't, and what you're learning. This prevents both arrogance (overlooking failures) and insecurity (dismissing successes).

One executive I worked with keeps a "confidence journal" with three simple prompts: "What did I do well today? What could I have done better? What will I focus on tomorrow?" This five-minute practice builds a cumulative confidence that isn't dependent on external feedback.

Third, **recovery practices**. Sustainable confidence requires sustainable energy. The shadows aren't just for work—they're for renewal. Physical movement, healthy eating, adequate sleep, meaningful connections, faith and spiritual enrichment, and activities that replenish your creative wellspring aren't luxuries. They're essential elements of your confidence infrastructure.

I've noticed that periods of lowest confidence often coincide with neglect of these fundamentals. The executive who skips workouts to handle a crisis, then finds themselves with brain fog or anxiety. The manager who sacrifices sleep to meet a deadline, then doubts their judgment or the quality of their work. The professional who cancels social connections to advance a project, then feels isolated and lonely.

What about those inevitable periods when the spotlight doesn't shine your way—when recognition is delayed, results are slow, or setbacks occur? This is when your confidence infrastructure truly proves its worth. That's when your investment in your own frameworks, practices, and opinion really pay off.

During these shadow periods, focus on process over outcomes. Maintain your deliberate practice. Double down on your reflection rituals. Protect your recovery practices. Remember that results lag behind effort, often significantly. The confidence you maintain in the shadows eventually creates results that are laudable.

After all, every spotlight moment you've ever witnessed—the athlete's championship performance, the executive's breakthrough presentation, the artist's stunning creation—was made possible by thousands of hours in the shadows. The confidence you witnessed wasn't created by the moment of recognition; it was revealed by it.

EXERCISE: THE SHADOW INVENTORY

1. List your three most recent "spotlight" successes.
2. For each, identify the specific shadow work that made it possible.
3. Rate your current investment (1-10) in each of the three confidence infrastructure elements: deliberate practice, reflection rituals, and recovery practices.
4. Choose your lowest-rated element and design one specific improvement you'll implement this week.

QUESTION TO REFLECT ON

What shadow work are you currently neglecting that, if invested in consistently, would make future spotlight moments almost inevitable?

FIRST STEP

Identify one skill central to your professional success. Create a deliberate practice routine that focuses specifically on the most challenging aspect of this skill, with clear parameters for time investment and feedback mechanisms. Commit to this practice for 30 days, regardless of whether anyone notices or recognizes your improvement.

LET'S STAY TOGETHER AND OTHER LESSONS FROM REALLY HARD TIMES

A personal reflection by

Remy Bernstein and Cooper Pickett

MANAGING PARTNERS OF TERRA, A DIGITAL
MARKETING AND COMMUNICATIONS AGENCY

Living through uncertainty is tough—leading through it is tougher.

The secrets are 1) show up, 2) speak up, and 3) grow despite it all.

When we look back at March 2020, there's still that twinge of disbelief—like, *"Did that really happen?"*

Practically overnight, Terra saw 50% of our business disappear. We'd poured years into building client relationships and refining our craft, only to watch the floor give out in real time. It was startling and sobering, and to be perfectly candid, we had no idea what the next month—or the next day—would bring.

But we knew one thing: we weren't going to pack it in.

And we certainly weren't going to abandon our people.

This is the story of how we navigated the most uncertain period our business has faced, and how those turbulent months reshaped who we are as leaders and as a company. It's also a testament to what you can accomplish with open communication, creative thinking, and a belief in your team. Because we did it.

We're not here to brag or to offer up a how-to manual. Instead, we want to share how we stumbled, recalibrated, and, in the process, found our footing—together.

Showing Up (Especially When It's Hard)

The earliest days of the pandemic are seared into our memory because it felt like a constant cycle of bad news. Public events and conferences were canceled.

Our hospitality and travel clients put entire marketing budgets on hold. New business leads dried up.

The question that kept us awake was: *What now?*

We'll be honest: it was tempting to slip into survival mode, to just keep our heads down and hope the storm would pass. But that wasn't really an option if we intended to stick around.

Instead, we adopted a simple motto that guided us every day: *Just show up.*

- Show up to the (then virtual) office with your camera on.
- Show up for internal meetings—no matter how small or trivial.
- Show up for each other in Slack, in text messages, in quick 15-minute phone calls to check in on people's well-being.
- Show up for our clients who still had pressing needs and wanted fresh ideas on how to stay relevant when the world was stuck at home.

Our "showing up" policy was less about maintaining a perfect professional façade—plenty of us wore sweatpants on Zoom calls—and more about making ourselves consistently available. We figured if we were around, if we listened, and if we kept the lines of communication open, we could adapt to the situation as it evolved. For us, that meant letting people ask hard questions—questions we couldn't always answer perfectly—and encouraging the honest exchange of concerns and solutions.

Radical Honesty in Communication

From the beginning, we believed strongly that our team deserved to understand the state of the business—both the successes and the mounting challenges. While it might have been easier for us to shield them from terrifying revenue projections, we chose to keep everyone informed. *This is what we know, this is what we don't know, and here are the possible outcomes.*

Sometimes it was a bit scary: we'd hop on our weekly all-hands call and, instead of typical updates, we'd walk the team through our finances, the conversations we were having with worried clients, and the reality that the next few months would be tough.

Yet a remarkable thing happened. Rather than panic or lose faith, people rolled up their sleeves. They asked what else they could do to help.

- Could they take on additional client calls?
- Could they propose new service offerings that might help us weather the storm?
- Could they reuse existing brand assets to create something fresh and relevant?

Being transparent about the precarious situation of our business gave people a chance to step up in ways we never anticipated. That spirit of ownership and innovation turned out to be one of our biggest advantages.

Resisting Layoffs and Reaping the Rewards

One difficult reality was that many agencies like ours were forced to trim down. We watched as talented friends and peers lost their jobs. Some would call it a "necessary evil." There was certainly plenty of industry chatter indicating that layoffs were the norm, and that preserving capital was the only way forward.

But we decided early on that we weren't letting anyone go. That's a gamble in a pandemic. It meant accepting potentially razor-thin margins and paying ourselves less for a while. But in our minds, our team was our most important asset, and the trust we'd built together was not easily replaceable. If we dismantled it to save a few dollars in the short term, how would we rebuild when things turned around?

That commitment was not easy or glamorous. We stayed up at night crunching numbers. We had heart-to-heart conversations with department heads about how to keep everyone busy and fulfilled. But we never regretted it.

In fact, as soon as the economy began to turn and new clients came knocking, we had a full roster of motivated people ready to get to work. That continuity fueled our next phase of growth, and it sparked a deep sense of loyalty we still see today. Having come through a crisis without losing each other, we appreciated our culture in a new way and built an unshakable sense of camaraderie.

Investing in Ourselves: The Cobbler's Shoes

There's a running joke in creative agencies that your own brand is the last thing on the list. You're so busy polishing everyone else's shoes, you never get around to your own. When the pandemic reduced our workload significantly, we suddenly had some extra time. Instead of telling our designers and strategists to sit idle, we gave them the go-ahead to tackle the rebrand we had been talking about for two years.

We decided to reimagine everything: our website, our pitch decks, our social presence. We didn't do this purely for aesthetics—it was an investment in ourselves. We wanted to articulate who we are in a more compelling way. We wanted to speak directly to future clients who might find us online. Most importantly, we wanted to instill in the entire agency the idea that *our own brand is valuable and worthy of care.*

Looking back, that decision changed our trajectory. The rebrand was successful beyond our hopes, driving new leads and new conversations. But more than that, it established a deep institutional commitment to continuously refining and investing in our own brand. We still block out time for "internal marketing" projects every quarter—just as we do for major client launches. That discipline has led to a consistent, recognizable identity and a steady stream of inbound interest from clients who first encounter us online.

Evolving Our Services to Meet the Moment

Working in marketing means you're constantly tuned in to the cultural undercurrents shaping consumer behavior—and 2020 gave us a tidal wave. People were stuck at home, glued to their smartphones for connection, comfort, and entertainment. For any business that wanted to reach them, social advertising was suddenly a necessity, not a nice-to-have. And so, we did something that felt almost counterintuitive in a crisis: we expanded our services.

Where we once simply offered paid media support as an add-on, we built an entire specialized practice around social advertising strategies. We created new team roles and partnerships. We hosted free webinars for businesses suddenly scrambling to pivot online. We launched pilot programs for small budgets, helping them test new channels without risking precious capital. By leaning into a rapidly shifting market, we not only kept Terra afloat—we created a new, robust, revenue stream that's still thriving today.

This shift forced us to be students, too. We pored over analytics and tested new creative concepts. We collaborated with brand partners to figure out what resonated with socially distanced audiences. That willingness to learn on the fly proved invaluable, and it reminded us of our original promise to each other and our team: keep showing up, keep adapting, and keep creating.

The Strength of Shared Commitment

Throughout this entire journey, one of our most important assets has been our partnership. People often warn that going into business with a friend can wreck both the business and the friendship. For us, it's been the opposite. We met years ago, became close friends, and then discovered we had complementary skills and a shared vision. The pressures of 2020—and beyond—tested our bond in every possible way but ultimately strengthened it.

Part of what kept us aligned was honest conversation. We had plenty of moments of friction—late-night calls about finances, heated debates about a risky new venture or partnership. But we always came back to two questions: *Do we trust each other?* and *Are we still pulling in the same direction?* The answer was always "yes." We don't take that for granted. A lot of leadership stories celebrate the lone hero. We've learned that having someone in the trenches with you—someone who not only supports but challenges you—is an extraordinary advantage.

Lessons We Carry Forward

Five years later, we can see a lot of things more clearly. That sense of panic we felt in early 2020 has long since faded into memory, replaced by new client challenges and new expansions in our service offerings. But certain lessons are now part of our DNA:

1. **Show up, no matter what.** People notice when leadership is present, transparent, and willing to shoulder the emotional weight of a crisis.
2. **Communicate openly.** Even tough news is better shared than withheld. Trust and respect are built on honesty.
3. **Invest in your own brand.** If you don't believe in your own worth, why would anyone else?
4. **Stay nimble.** Each challenge can be an opportunity if you're open to re-thinking how you work and what you offer.
5. **Never undervalue partnership and team.** Whether it's your business partner or your employees, relationships are the backbone of success.

We won't claim that any of this was easy or that we have it all figured out. We're grateful that we kept the team intact and came out of the pandemic stronger—better connected, more confident in our brand, and more excited than ever to keep building. If someone had told us in 2019 that we'd lose half our business and then end up growing exponentially the following year, we would have laughed them out of the room. Yet here we are.

Surviving a crisis isn't about perfection. It's about showing up day after day, owning the vulnerability of the moment, and trusting the people around you. We hope our story can be a testament to those principles. We're not special. We're just dedicated to doing the work we love, and to doing it alongside people we trust. And for us, that's a definition of success that no pandemic can take away.

ABOUT REMY BERNSTEIN AND COOPER PICKETT

Remy Bernstein, a partner at Terra, provides direct client strategy and project delivery across three offices on two continents. A member of the Forbes New York Business Council and a founding member of the Columbia University Startup Lab, he previously worked in the editorial departments at Publishers Weekly and S&P Global. Remy and the Terra team execute strategies focused on content creation, digital transformation, and brand marketing for clients.

Cooper Pickett, managing partner at Terra, provides leadership and technical vision for the firm's expansive practice as a global marketing agency built for the digital world. Terra's designers, writers, and marketers produce awarding winning, high performing digital properties and campaigns for industry leading companies and organizations.

Connect with Remy and Cooper at TerraHQ.com.

ASSESSMENT

PIERCE CAREER GUIDANCE, PRECISION, AND STRATEGY (GPS) QUIZ

Are you navigating your path with what I call "spatial intelligence?" Here's a check up on your guidance system, including as assessment of the precision, strategy, and foresight you're currently using. Spatial intelligence is much like a GPS system helping a driver stay on course, avoid obstacles, and anticipate upcoming challenges. It's essential in the fast paced, dynamic nature of your career management.

Instructions

Take the 15-point quiz designed to assess your spatial intelligence in the context of your career management. The questions will help identify if you are seeing the full field of play in your career or whether you're missing critical cues and patterns. Each question has five multiple choice answers, and some may have more than one correct answer, but you must choose only one answer. If you don't see an answer that suits you perfectly, choose the one that's closest to your ideal answer. Note that the grading key follows the quiz—but don't peek before completing all 15 questions!

Spatial Intelligence Quiz

1 How often do you seek feedback from peers, managers, or clients about your performance, beyond what is required by your organization in regular reviews?

A. Regularly
B. Often
C. Occasionally
D. Rarely
E. Never

2 When a new challenge arises, how likely are you to spend significant time anticipating potential obstacles before they become a problem?

A. Always
B. Frequently
C. Sometimes
D. Infrequently
E. Never

3 How often do you reevaluate your professional goals, objectives, and strategies in response to changes in your company or industry?

A. Monthly
B. Quarterly
C. Annually
D. Only when told to do so
E. I don't

4 How aware are you of the political landscape or power dynamics within your company?

A. Very aware, I actively monitor it
B. Somewhat aware, I keep it in mind
C. Neutral, I notice it but don't focus on it
D. Mostly unaware unless directly affected
E. Completely unaware

5 How do you react when your decision or strategy is challenged by someone more experienced or with more authority?

A. I carefully consider their perspective

B. I seek clarification and try to learn from it

C. I stay firm in my position

D. I avoid confrontation and move on

E. I feel threatened or defensive

6 How frequently do you reach out to different departments or teams to understand their perspective on companywide issues?

A. Weekly

B. Monthly

C. Quarterly

D. Annually

E. Rarely or never

7 How well do you manage to adjust your communication style to suit different types of personalities within your organization?

A. Very well, I adapt easily

B. Okay, but sometimes I forget

C. I try, but not always successfully

D. I find it difficult to adapt

E. I don't adapt my communication style

8 How often do you "zoom out" from your day-to-day work to assess the broader market or industry trends affecting your business?

A. At least weekly, I see it as essential to my job

B. Once or twice each month, it's interesting and useful

C. Quarterly or when I attend our local industry association meetings

D. Annually or when go to a conference

E. I don't

9 How do you react to unexpected changes in strategy or direction from senior leadership?

    A. I adapt quickly and proactively seek out what's ahead

    B. I seek clarity when there's a change and adjust accordingly if needed

    C. I follow the new plan but find it irritating that change happens without warning

    D. I struggle to keep up with rapid changes and try to fit in what I'm already doing

    E. I resist the change

10 How much effort do you put into maintaining relationships with key stakeholders (both internal and external)?

    A. A great deal, I'm proactive in relationship-building

    B. A lot, I maintain good relationships

    C. Some, but not as much as I should

    D. Not much, I let relationships form naturally

    E. Very little, I don't see it as a priority

11 When you face a setback, how quickly do you assess the root cause and pivot to a new strategy?

    A. Immediately or as soon as possible

    B. After some reflection and especially when a manager brings it to my attention

    C. After a period of doubt or frustration or when I can't ignore the problem

    D. I often get stuck in the setback and can't seem to climb out easily

    E. I rarely analyze the root cause, I just handle problems as they come

12 How likely are you to anticipate and navigate conflicts with colleagues before they escalate into bigger issues?

    A. Very likely, I see conflicts coming early

    B. Likely, I notice warning signs

    C. Sometimes, but I'm often too late

    D. Rarely, conflicts catch me off guard

    E. Never, I avoid colleague conflicts

13 How frequently do you take steps to ensure you're not blindsided by market or client shifts (e.g., client satisfaction, operational issues)?

    A. Very frequently, I stay ahead of changes

    B. Frequently, I monitor regularly

    C. Occasionally, but I react after the fact

    D. Rarely, I often don't see shifts until it's too late

    E. Never, I deal with issues as they come

14 When working on a major project, how often do you identify and mitigate risks early in the process?

    A. Always or almost always

    B. Often

    C. Sometimes

    D. Rarely

    E. Never

15 How aware are you of informal networks within your company that might influence decision-making that impacts you (beyond the obvious official hierarchies)?

    A. Very aware, I engage with these networks

    B. Somewhat aware, I observe them

    C. Neutral, I don't pay much attention

    D. Unaware unless it directly affects me

    E. Completely unaware

Grading Key

Each question is graded on a scale of 1 to 5. The higher the score, the stronger the person's spatial intelligence.

A = 5

B = 4

C = 3

D = 2

E = 1

Scoring Guide

70-75 points: Exceptional Spatial Intelligence—You have an outstanding ability to see the full field of play, anticipate obstacles, and navigate your career with finesse.

55-69 points: Strong Spatial Intelligence—You are generally very aware and adaptive, with occasional blind spots to improve.

40-54 points: Moderate Spatial Intelligence—You have some awareness but may miss critical cues or fail to anticipate major shifts.

25-39 points: Limited Spatial Intelligence—You often find yourself reacting to issues rather than anticipating them and may frequently be caught off guard.

Below 25 points: Low Spatial Intelligence—You are often blindsided by career challenges and may struggle to navigate the complexities of your career environment effectively.

Set Up Your Spatial Intelligence Action Plan

Now you have a good sense of where you stand in terms of your ability to navigate complex, fast-paced, or politically nuanced environments. You've also identified areas where coaching, training, mentoring, and guided experiences can enhance your spatial intelligence.

When you review the questions and your responses, what three areas do you most want to improve?

ASSESSMENT

PIERCE LEADERSHIP ELEVATION PLAYBOOK

A s you prepare to elevate your game in the workplace, coaching may be key to your leveling up. Great coaches ask great questions—so this question guide will help you evaluate your current coach or get ready for coaching if you haven't yet started.

This playbook is organized for the typical progression of an employee, from the time they enter the corporate environment as a rookie, through different levels of leadership. Hence, it can become your very own playbook as you seek to advance from your current role to your ideal position.

No matter where you are in your career, any of the questions may appeal to you. For example, even if you've been promoted a few times, you may have skipped a key skill or need a bit of remediation or refresher. Each question homes in on growth, strategy, and actionable steps for personal and professional development. Consider how you might customize a question for yourself, specifically to help you elevate from where you are now to what you are hoping to achieve next.

Instructions

1. Review each question, customizing it as you like to suit your circumstances.
2. Put a check next to each question that sparks your interest.

3. Review the questions you've check marked and choose your top five questions.
4. Rank order your choices by their priority for your career success (with #1 being the most important and #5 being the lowest priority).
5. Consider taking this list to your coach or using it to coach yourself to success.

Rookies (New Employees)

Typically, rookies are employees just entering the workforce. They are focused on learning, integrating into the company culture, and gaining foundational skills. If you're a rookie, what questions would you like to discuss and have firm, clear answers to? How would you customize these for your particular situation?

The Coach Asks:

1. What specific skills or knowledge do you feel you need to develop in order to perform better in your role?
2. How confident are you in understanding the company culture and its expectations?
3. How comfortable do you feel asking for help or guidance when you are unsure about something?
4. What strategies would you like to explore to manage stress and workload as you adapt to your new responsibilities?
5. How well are you balancing your personal and professional life as you start your career?
6. What does success in the first year of your career look like to you, and how can coaching help you achieve it?
7. What areas do you think would benefit from mentorship, and how do you envision integrating mentorship into your growth plan?

Major Leaguers (Employees 3-5 Years Into Their Careers)

Typically, risers are employees beginning to solidify their roles and ambitions but may face challenges around career growth, getting noticed, and managing increasing responsibilities. What questions would you like to discuss and develop firm, clear answers to? How would you customize these?

The Coach Asks:

1. How clear are you about your career trajectory within the company, and what would you like to explore further?
2. What do you find most rewarding and most frustrating about your current role?
3. How effectively do you feel you are managing your time and priorities, and what improvements would you like to see?
4. What feedback have you received from supervisors or peers, and how would you like to apply that to your development?
5. How well do you handle constructive criticism, and in what ways could coaching help you develop resilience?
6. How comfortable do you feel advocating for your own professional development (e.g., seeking promotions, raises, new roles)?
7. What leadership or advanced skills would you like to develop in preparation for future promotions or opportunities?

Team Captains (New Supervisors)

Typically, team captains are transitioning from being part of the team to leading the team. They are learning to navigate leadership responsibilities and team dynamics. What coaching questions would you like to discuss and develop firm, clear answers to? How would you customize these?

The Coach Asks:

1. How well do you feel you are transitioning from an individual contributor role or team mate to a supervisory role?
2. What challenges have you faced in managing former peers, and what approaches have worked or failed?
3. How confident are you in your ability to delegate tasks while maintaining accountability?
4. How do you ensure that your team is motivated and aligned with the company's goals, and how can coaching enhance this?
5. What leadership style do you think you naturally gravitate toward, and how do you plan to adjust it for different team members?

6. How comfortable are you providing feedback, both positive and constructive, and what areas of this skill do you want to improve?
7. In what areas do you feel unsupported as a new supervisor, and how can coaching help you address those gaps?

Head Coaches (New Managers)

Typically, head coaches are stepping into a broader role, managing teams, projects, and often other supervisors. They are responsible for larger-scale results. What coaching questions would you like to discuss and develop firm, clear answers to? How would you customize these?

The Coach Asks:

1. How confident are you in setting team goals and aligning them with the organization's strategic objectives?
2. What challenges do you face in balancing hands-on involvement with giving your team autonomy?
3. How effectively are you managing cross-functional communication and ensuring collaboration between departments?
4. What aspects of your management style do you feel need refinement, and how would you like to work on those?
5. How do you manage the balance between operational efficiency and fostering innovation within your team?
6. What specific leadership qualities do you admire, and how can coaching help you develop those within yourself?
7. How are you handling the increased pressure to deliver results, and what strategies are you interested in exploring to manage stress?

Veterans (Mid-level Managers Seeking Senior VP Roles)

Typically, these managers are highly experienced but may feel stuck or ready for the next level. They seek to polish their leadership abilities and position themselves for senior leadership roles or going out on their own. What coaching questions would you like to discuss and develop firm, clear answers to? How would you customize these?

The Coach Asks:

1. How confident are you that your current leadership style is preparing you for a senior-level role?
2. What areas of your decision-making do you feel could be more strategic, and how do you approach long-term planning?
3. How are you actively developing your team to reflect leadership qualities and skills that support your upward mobility?
4. In what areas do you need more visibility within the organization to advance your career?
5. How do you handle feedback or performance reviews at this level, and what do you want to work on regarding your response to feedback?
6. What challenges do you face in building influence among senior leaders, and how can coaching help you improve your executive presence?
7. How are you ensuring that your professional development continues, despite feeling "seasoned" in your role?

Champions (Top Leadership Just Below C-Suite)

Typically, these individuals are one step away from top leadership. They may need to refine their vision, increase their influence, and prepare for the highest level of responsibility. What coaching questions would you like to discuss and develop firm, clear answers to? How would you customize these?

The Coach Asks:

1. How well do you feel your current vision aligns with the organization's long-term goals, and where do you see opportunities for refinement?
2. How confident are you in leading organizational change, and what areas would you like to strengthen?
3. What strategies have you implemented to influence the executive team and how can coaching help you become a more persuasive leader?
4. How well do you navigate political dynamics within the organization, and where do you need support in managing relationships at the highest level?
5. How do you ensure that your leadership approach inspires the next generation of leaders while maintaining top-level performance?

6. How do you balance long-term strategic vision with the day-to-day operational pressures at your level?
7. How prepared do you feel for transitioning to a C-suite role, and what would you like to focus on in your leadership development to make that jump?

Develop your own customized Pierce Leadership Elevation Playbook

While the standard playbook associates specific roles with certain questions that address the varying levels of career progression, now you can pick from any level. Make sure to consider how you want to tailor coaching topics to reflect your unique experience, challenges, and aspirations.

1. What are your top five in rank order (from most important to lowest priority)?
2. What additional questions or support would you like from a coach or mentor?

FORTUNE FAVORS THE PREPARED MIND.

—LOUIS PASTEUR

PART III
THRIVING AGAINST THE ODDS

*The best way to avenge yourself
is to not be like that.*

—Marcus Aurelius

11

FISHING, HUNTING, GATHERING, COOKING, AND CLEANING UP

"Teach someone to fish, and they'll never go hungry." You've heard this little nugget of wisdom before. It sounds profound, doesn't it? A perfect bite-sized morsel of career advice that fits neatly on an inspirational poster in your HR department's conference room. Fundamentally this well-meaning phrase is a mean-spirited admonition. Don't just give fish to hungry people, or they'll never learn how to fend for themselves.

Like most simplified solutions to complex problems, it's easy to repeat and fundamentally wrong.

Let's get real about today's workplace

You're not alone on a riverbank with a makeshift fishing rod, trying to catch your next meal. You're in a sophisticated ecosystem where success depends on collaboration, specialized skills, and understanding your role within a larger system. Even if you work remotely from home, you are not alone, starving on a riverbank with a piece of bamboo tied to a fibrous string from a fallen leaf.

The purpose of most workplaces is to successfully use a wealth of sophisticated tools they provide and engage successfully with your manager, department team, or a cross-functional group to meet company goals rapidly. While everyone is to some extent an individual contributor, if you approach work as feeding yourself and no one else, you can expect hostility on your next 360 performance evaluation. Or worse.

Here's the uncomfortable truth

Not everyone is meant to fish. Some excel at research and gathering resources. Others are best at hunting down new opportunities or clients. Some are picked to prepare and enhance the deals that have been won. And yes, someone must clean up the mess so the whole operation doesn't collapse under its own waste.

Even in a tribe, not everyone is meant to fish. Some people are meant to gather wood for a fire so we're not always eating raw fish. Others are meant to provide variety by way of hunting down a beast or wild grown quinoa in the forest. Some are meant to prepare the protein sources, maybe flavor them up a bit, and cook them. And still others are meant to clean up after the meal so we can still use the campsite without bears and ants eating us alive.

In other words, when you are working with others, your value doesn't come from doing everything equally well. It comes from excelling in your role while appreciating how it connects to everyone else's. The modern workplace isn't about self-sufficiency—it's about interdependence. People need to rely on you to do your part so they can feel secure focusing on theirs.

What no one tells you in those career development seminars: You will likely spend significant portions of your career not enjoying aspects of your job, the people you work with, the expectations placed on you, or your compensation.

And when you look around at what others get to do or how much they make, your instinct will be to say, "That's not fair."

You're right. It isn't fair. Nothing about work is.

That's your first lesson in thriving against the odds: Accept this reality every morning before you badge into the building or sign into your workstation. As Tom Hanks' character so eloquently put it in *A League of Their Own*: "There's no crying in baseball."

No successful organization wants Wendy Whiner. Debbie Downer. Todd Tattletale. Wilford WhatAboutMe. These characters might have gotten participation trophies in youth sports, but the professional world operates differently.

MAKING SENSE OF ROLES IN THE WORKPLACE

1

FISHING: STRATEGISTS & VISIONAIRIES

Big-picture thinkers who identify opportunities and set direction.

2

HUNTING: GO-GETTERS & CLOSERS

Action-driven individuals who chase goals and close deals.

3

GATHERING: RESOURCE COORDINATORS

Team members who organize, collect, and support execution.

4

COOKING: IMPLEMENTERS & PROBLEM-SOLVERS

The doers who transform raw materials into finished results.

5

CLEANING UP: OPTIMIZERS & EVALUATORS

Those who refine, improve, and ensure long-term success.

6

COLLABORATE

- Not everyone does everything, but everyone contributes.
- Respect for colleagues, managers, and clients builds relationships and resilience.
- Take the opportunity to master each role so you become an empathetic, well-rounded leader.

Work isn't high school

There's no award for "most likely to succeed" or "best smile." Look at the most successful people in business—Bill Gates, Mark Zuckerberg, even the fallen Elizabeth Holmes. None won popularity contests. And those glamorous influencers you envy? They spend most of their day in bathrooms applying makeup or isolated hallways performing dance moves, then editing footage in the dark (yes, even with AI).

Nothing in your education prepared you for the realities of work—except work itself.

You'll never have your "dream job" because once you get it, you'll discover it involves grueling hours, demanding people, and relentless pressure. You may reach the summit only to find your personal relationships have withered while a board of directors holds your feet to the fire. That's when your mastery of all aspects—fishing, hunting, gathering, cooking, and cleaning up—will face the ultimate test.

Why you work (beyond paying rent)

You're not just working to pay bills. You're in the arena to increase your mastery—not just of technical skills, but of the human dimensions of professional life. You're there to do hard things—mastering challenges that test you cognitively, socially, emotionally, physically, and spiritually.

This crucible builds something far more valuable than a resume: resilience. Not just the will to pursue rewards, but the will to persevere when life throws you curveballs with no warning and bad timing.

To truly understand this confounding truth: after the worst days come the best days. It's a cycle. Just. Like. Life.

Work offers more than paychecks and promotions. It's the proving ground for a life well-lived. For making hard choices when all options seem terrible. For joining with others to overcome challenges that would overwhelm any individual, finding unexpected strength, courage, and even joy in the process.

When you respect your work—and everyone connected to it from managers to colleagues to clients to suppliers—you respect yourself.

Whether your current position becomes a stepping stone or an unexpected dead end, mastering what's in front of you always pays dividends. Even if that opportunity ends "unfairly," the capabilities you've developed remain yours to carry forward.

EXERCISE: THE ROLE INVENTORY

For each workplace role below, identify when you've performed it, what you learned, and how it contributed to your professional development:

1. Fishing or Hunting (seeking new opportunities, clients, or resources)
2. Gathering (collecting and organizing information or materials)
3. Cooking (transforming raw inputs into valuable outputs)
4. Cleaning Up (resolving problems, managing aftermath, maintaining systems)

QUESTION TO REFLECT ON

Which of these roles makes you most uncomfortable,
and what capabilities might you develop by leaning
into that discomfort rather than avoiding it?

FIRST STEP

Identify one aspect of your current role that feels misaligned with your strengths or preferences. For the next week, approach it not as a burden but as deliberate practice in building your professional versatility.

Reclaim Your
Inner Power

When you measure your worth only by your paycheck, you lose sight of who you are

Set goals beyond work – target personal development, health, spiritual life, and relationships

Forgive yourself and others who judged you only by your external achievements

Build your mind and character while you build your career and financial stability

You win when you decide who you truly want to be – and become that person!

YOU CAN DO iT!

PERSEVERANCE AND OPTIMISM FROM THE FARM TO FINANCIAL SERVICES

A personal reflection by

Brian Waelti

FINANCIAL SERVICES EXECUTIVE

If you push through the storms, you'll see sunshine again

Stay connected to good people and good values

For this farm kid from Wisconsin, persistence is a way of life. Not a choice. Not an option. Not just when you feel strong, well-rested, or had enough to eat. An enduring life-lesson from my childhood is to push through every day despite snow, heat, rain, wind.

I've approached my 25+ year career in financial services with that persistence, putting one foot in front of the other. By tackling each seemingly overwhelming obstacle, business problem, critical feedback, and challenge with a "you got this" attitude—I've found a way to get to the next milestone. I had a leader once tell me; "If you're doing what is right, and you don't win, make a new argument and another and another, until you get to the right solution."

When I reflect on how much I relied on persistence during my career, it's clear that I lacked rigorous and purpose-driven career-planning—which would have led to fewer obstacles. That's something I hope you can glean from *Unshakable Confidence*. Tenacity alone is not enough for enduring success, because some events will be beyond your ability to control, much less gut through. You need multiple strengths include a flexible, growth-oriented mindset. To steer your way through crisis and opportunities, your plan should be to nurture a network of reliable connections, create balance, be smart with your money so you have security, and stay current on your skills. Strategic thinking now will prevent you from being blindsided or empty-handed in the future.

Because setbacks are inevitable, I want to share what they have meant in my life and how I approached and defined winning.

First, setbacks are a fact. Shake off any negative connotations about that word "setback." They are a fact of life in a career. Second, setbacks do not have to define you or your career. If you prepare for them, you do more than bounce back, you can bounce forward.

Twice, because of forces outside my control, I was caught in a "RIF," a reduction of force—let go. The first RIF came after I had spent 19 years with a large bank. Ultimately, that led me to a great job with a good firm. The time in between jobs was a blessing, because I could recharge after so many years at one firm. Having confidence in my ability, the strength of my network and friends, and knowing nature has a way of working things out, motivated me every day as I navigated that job search.

Success at the next firm came at a cost. While I enjoyed professional success, there was a huge void because I was away from friends and family. After 20+ years in a community, starting anew was harder than I realized. I simply was ready to embrace that level of change and live for just the job itself.

In my next position, I joined one of the major consulting firms. It seemed like the perfect decision: great name and great location, but unfortunately the promise of great work went unfulfilled.

For the last several months, with 19 years at one firm and then three firms in nine years, I've had to reassess what really matters to me. What does success and personal fulfillment really look like? This is where my farm bred perseverance really does pay off. In making this decision, I continue to approach each day with vigor and optimism.

In large part, I've redefined winning so it reflects my goals *and* my values. At each interlude between corporate jobs, I remained surrounded by friends. I benefited from having had financial success. And I knew that for me, personal happiness and satisfaction must be part of the career equation.

You may define success differently. Deciding what matters in your career is essential to do as early and perhaps often as possible—because you need a strategic way to go about managing the ups and downs that are part of life. For you, success might be immense wealth, the biggest house, exotic travel, or significant recognition. It might be other types of achievement. It might be security and the comfort of friends and family.

Once you set your own definition of success, consider what it takes for you to weather the inevitable setbacks. Set up your foundation—what you need in your life—so you can confidently and optimistically say that no matter what, the sun will come up tomorrow and with it, new opportunities for you.

A few thoughts to sustain you:

1. Surround yourself personally and professionally with great people. Lift each other up and give honest feedback. There's an adage that says you're the average of your five closest friends. Keep good people close and stick by them.

   Sidenote: Recently, I had a summer where my group of friends averaged $0 in income—remind each other, it gets better!

2. Reflect on the values you hold true—whether you got them growing up or discovered them later in life. Let your values guide your decision making. While I don't have regrets—there are things I wish I could do over. Don't let regret eat away at your confidence. Remember that we make the best decisions we can with the information we have at the time. What happens after that can't always be foreseen.

   Sidenote: First rule I learned in college was that it all "evens out" in the end. I believe that to be true today. No regrets.

3. Setbacks and obstacles come in many forms and often aren't predictable. They might come from places you don't even know existed or couldn't see. They become experiences that give us perspective.

   Sidenote: I used to think that everyone was a team player, because I am a team player. It took some shocking experiences for me to realize some folks have nothing more than their self-interest in mind. Keep your eyes wide open.

4. Exit with grace. One of my personal rules is to maintain friendships with quality people regardless of a firm's decision to let you go—even when those people participated in that decision. In my case, I knew the RIF was just business and wasn't a reflection on me. When a firm makes a strategic

pivot and eliminates an entire division, you can't take that personally or take it out on the bearer of bad news. By acting respectfully throughout the process, you can re-visit new opportunities when they occur. The next opportunity with that firm might be an even better fit and more lucrative.

Sidenote: I am actually taking another swing of the bat at a former firm, interviewing for a role that seems interesting and fun. Had I left with a chip on my shoulder, or a grudge, I would have been put on the "do not hire ever again list" (all firms have this list).

In summary: Surround yourself with good people, hold fast to your values, watch out for obstacles, and have no regrets. Wake up with a positive outlook, good intentions, and act accordingly. Expect to have days when optimism is hard to find and take the time to reflect or even mourn what aches.

How do you want to wake up every morning? Despite wind, rain, snow, or sun; put a smile on and start another day knowing it will always get better.

ABOUT BRIAN WAELTI

Brian Waelti is a passionate leader with extensive experience shaping and executing corporate strategy, driving transformational change, and building high-performing teams in wealth management. With over 20 years of success in financial services, developing and implementing strategies that deliver measurable growth for financial advisors, he has successfully led cross-enterprise initiatives, managing complex projects and collaborating with diverse stakeholders to achieve organizational objectives. Brian was recently featured in Franklin Templeton's The Future of Investing: 2024/25 Edition, honored as one of the 87 leading thinkers interviewed in the investment management industry. He has been recognized in the industry and by numerous firms for outstanding leadership.

12

FORGIVENESS AND FORGETFULNESS: THE TWIN PILLARS OF RESILIENCE

What gives you power also takes it away. Let's talk about pride. When you take immense pride in your accomplishments, you risk being defined by *what* you achieve, not *how* you achieved it. The external validation becomes the drug, while the transformative journey—the part that actually builds unshakable confidence—gets forgotten like yesterday's news.

Here's a brutal truth about thriving against the odds

If your sense of power comes from a title under your name on a business card or your LinkedIn profile, you've willingly imprisoned yourself. The warden? Whoever gave you that title. If you're waiting to feel powerful until you get that "prestigious" position and six or seven figure salary, you're standing in line for someone else's permission to matter. What a tragic exchange: trading your self-worth for temporary external validation.

Every time you let a job, promotion, or deal become the measure of who you are, you're not just giving someone the power to evaluate your work. You're handing them the keys to your self-esteem. How could that possibly be what you intended when you set out to build a career?

It's like volunteering to be a yo-yo, swinging up and down at someone else's whim. Or the cartoon character in a tiny cart while someone else controls the joystick, sending you crashing into walls or barely making it over obstacles.

Would you knowingly sign up to be someone's puppet? Of course not.

Yet when ambition grows without equal attention to your values and character, you surrender control over the very meaning of your life. This surrender is the opposite of thriving—it's merely surviving at someone else's pleasure.

The meaning of life isn't found in metrics with dollar signs or percentages. It's not your position on an org chart or the number of people reporting to you. These are corporate constructs designed to extract maximum value from your talent while giving you minimum control over your destiny.

Your role in business is not a reflection of your value as a human being. We've been conditioned to define ourselves by title and company whenever someone asks what we do—like prisoners of war solemnly giving name, rank, and serial number to hostile interrogators.

It's easy to forget that work is simply meant to be the economic engine of your life. Your contribution deserves fair compensation—sometimes you'll get less than you deserve, occasionally more. At its best, your paycheck is just a rough exchange for what an organization gets from you, with the company ensuring its expenses are covered and shareholders rewarded.

When you lose this perspective—when you believe a bigger title or salary makes you more important or powerful—you lose yourself, even if you get everything you thought you wanted.

Thriving against the odds requires both forgiveness and forgetfulness

First, forgiveness. Your employer has a vested interest in this confusion. The more you define yourself by your job, the better for those who sign your checks. But it's not just your employer who put work on this pedestal.

From childhood, parents asked what you wanted to "be" when you grew up. They weren't hoping you'd say, "I want to be resilient, compassionate, and filled with purpose." They wanted to hear occupation titles, preferably prestigious ones. Schools reinforced this, defining you by your major rather than helping you discover your authentic strengths and values.

Forgive them all

Forgive employers, parents, teachers, friends, and strangers who wanted you to define yourself by what you do. Forgive those who say "I'm so proud of you" only when you get a new job, title, or raise.

Most importantly, forgive yourself. You've outsourced your self-worth because you were trained to define yourself in terms that made it easy for others to categorize you. Using job titles is simpler than articulating what lives in your heart and soul—that's too intimate, too complex, too messy.

That is, until the setback comes. When you lose your job, miss that promotion, or watch peers advance while you stall, you discover that pride indeed goes before a fall.

This is where forgetfulness becomes crucial to thriving against the odds.

Some people never recover from career falls. The tumble leaves them afraid to rise again, their ego—which was misplaced in others' hands—too brittle to withstand the impact.

Some professional athletes take one hit too many and never return to the field. Others, like the seemingly indestructible Tom Brady did for decades, keep making comebacks.

What's the difference between a career-ending setback and a powerful comeback? Using the recovery time to gain perspective. Reevaluating work's proper place in your life's hierarchy of meaning. Forgetting the false lessons about where your value truly resides.

This is how you thrive against the odds that constantly push against you in corporate America. Never forget that what you do is not who you are. Never sell your self-esteem when you submit your resume or negotiate a deal.

As you pick yourself up—which you will do repeatedly, even in a "successful" career—shake off the belief that anyone ever truly held your worth in their hands. Forget what you were indoctrinated to believe about power and prestige. Put work in its proper place.

This deliberate forgetting of false values, combined with forgiveness for yourself and others, creates the space for genuine resilience. It builds the foundation for that unshakable confidence that withstands any corporate storm.

Only then do you become truly powerful, with authentic pride in yourself rather than just your accomplishments. Only then can you thrive, not just despite the odds, but because you've changed the game entirely.

EXERCISE: RECLAIM YOUR WORTH

1. List three moments when you felt your self-worth rise or fall based solely on external professional validation
2. For each instance, identify what core personal value was actually being expressed through your work (e.g., creativity, leadership, problem-solving)
3. Create a personal definition of success that centers on these values rather than external markers
4. Identify one action you'll take this week to honor these values, regardless of professional recognition

QUESTION TO REFLECT ON

What parts of your professional identity would remain intact
if your job, title, and company disappeared tomorrow?

FIRST STEP

Write down three non-work-related strengths or qualities that make you valuable beyond your professional role. Place this list somewhere you'll see it daily—especially before important work meetings or evaluations.

NAVIGATING BETRAYALS, BREAKTHROUGHS, AND EVERYTHING BETWEEN

A personal reflection by

John Pierce

My dear friend George called me today. George's smart, connected, and generous. You'd think that would be a winning combination. It's not. At least not always—and therein lies a lesson.

A while back, George took a call from a former colleague, Mike, who was job hunting. George extended himself—made the introductions, vouched for Mike's talents, and helped him get hired at George's firm. Then, through a combination of solid work and favorable winds, Mike got promoted. Now he's George's boss.

Everything seemed fine until George heard through the grapevine that Mike had been systematically downplaying George's knowledge, experience, and contributions. While it's not exactly shocking when a boss claims credit for a subordinate's brilliance, it cuts deeper when the person doing the harm is someone you helped out. The sting is particularly sharp when you hear it second-hand. You weren't there to witness it, so was it really as bad as reported? And even if it was precisely that bad, what's your next move?

The real question is, when something happens to you, whether an ambush or an opportunity, what do you do? A flood of options typically races through your mind, but you might not be thinking clearly about them or their ripple effects. Do you schedule that confrontational meeting to clear the air? Do you simply swallow it and move on? Do you become more strategic about documenting and broadcasting your accomplishments so you're less vulnerable to having your contributions erased?

A similar dilemma might occur when something fantastic happens or when inspiration strikes. Do you immediately march into your boss's office with your grand vision? Do you quietly begin orchestrating your next career chess move? Do you keep your powder dry until you've built something more substantial?

Here's where sounding boards become invaluable. When you're nursing a brilliant idea, facing a workplace crisis, contemplating a major professional pivot, or deciding whether to extend yourself for someone else, you benefit enormously from engaging with a trustworthy, intelligent, insightful, and experienced individual who can offer an unvarnished assessment of your options.

Don't go it alone. Find yourself a proper sounding board. This person must be wise, someone you genuinely respect, and capable of brutal honesty with you. They must also be unselfish, relatively unbiased, and—critically—a good listener. These qualities aren't easy to find in one package, but they're essential in someone serving as your sounding board. After they've truly heard you out, expect them to pose some uncomfortable questions. The best sounding boards slice through the noise, helping you distinguish between what's truly consequential versus what's merely interesting or nice-to-have.

As I do for friends and those I've mentored, coached, and led throughout my corporate journey, I served as George's sounding board when he faced his dilemma with Mike. My first question was straightforward: What's the downside of providing feedback to Mike or anyone involved? Politically, there would likely be fallout. Then, what's the upside? While it might clear the air and potentially prevent similar situations down the road, was the potential gain worth the risk?

Remember, a sounding board isn't there to make decisions for you but to help you think more clearly for yourself and add some context. Once you've worked through the problem, reviewed your thoughts, and achieved some emotional distance, reconnect with your sounding board. Make refinements together, so you're not navigating treacherous waters alone.

With an intelligent, experienced, and genuinely selfless sounding board in your corner, your plans will be exponentially stronger than anything you might cobble together in isolation. The corporate world is full of dilemmas—but with the right sounding board, you'll be prepared for them when they come your way!

13

THE ROCKSTAR, PODCASTER
AND YOU: DOING SOUND CHECKS

You know that moment when you think you've got a brilliant idea or you're facing a career dilemma that feels like a crossroads? Your first instinct is to "bounce it off someone." That's natural. But who you choose as your sounding board—and how you use them—might be the difference between thriving against the odds and crashing spectacularly.

Let's be honest: Most people pick sounding boards for all the wrong reasons. They choose someone who's available, someone who usually agrees with them, or someone they can easily manipulate into giving the validation they crave. Then they wonder why their "great idea" crashed and burned when they finally took it public.

Thriving in environments stacked against you requires something different. It demands finding sounding boards who will tell you what you need to hear, not what you want to hear. Think about what a sound engineer does for a rockstar or podcaster. They don't just amplify whatever comes through the mic—they filter out noise, balance levels, add appropriate effects, and ensure the final output resonates with the audience. Your ideal sounding board should do the same for your ideas and decisions.

How to get started

The first task of a good sound engineer is eliminating background noise. Your sounding board should help separate your core idea from the static of emotion, timing, and circumstance that might be clouding your judgment. Are you considering that transfer to another city because of the opportunity, or because you can't stand living near your in-laws? Are you thinking about going over your boss's head because the situation truly warrants it, or because you're still seething from last week's disagreement? And even if you're right—does senior leadership want to hear this from you?

A skilled engineer doesn't just clean up sound—they enhance it with effects that serve the performer's purpose. Similarly, your sounding board should help you model different ways to achieve your goal. They should expand your view beyond the limited options you initially see. One of the most overlooked choices they might suggest? Patience.

Even the best idea might need the right conditions before implementation

What timing would be optimal? Who should you approach first? How can you test sentiment with key stakeholders? Your sounding board should challenge you with these questions.

What you absolutely don't want is an echo chamber—someone who reflexively agrees with everything you say. Sometimes people endorse your plans simply to end the conversation or stay in your good graces. Junior colleagues, direct reports, or even friends might avoid conflict by cheering you on rather than critically assessing your ideas. That's not a sounding board; it's a mirror reflecting back what you already believe.

Get ready to speak and listen

When you've identified the right person, prepare to present your situation objectively. You've likely been marinating in this problem or idea for weeks, but they're hearing it for the first time. Distill the essential information, create space for them to probe deeper, and be prepared to practice your eventual approach based on their feedback.

Here's a formula for making these sessions productive when you're trying to thrive against long odds:

1. **Set the scene with three vital contextual factors.** For example: "My four-year anniversary with the firm is approaching. Despite consistent raises and positive evaluations, my title and responsibilities haven't changed. Meanwhile, I've acquired additional credentials specifically relevant to advancement."

2. **Present your dilemma or idea clearly.** For example: "If I'm not offered a promotion this cycle, I'm considering directly challenging my boss about why I remain in the same role while peers at other companies are advancing. I want to emphasize that maintaining career progression is important to me."

3. **Invite questions with a sounding board prompt.** For example: "What additional information would help you understand this situation better?"

4. **Request critical feedback explicitly.** For example: "Where are the weaknesses in my thinking? What factors am I overlooking? How might this approach be perceived?"

Remember, this isn't collaborative decision-making—it's your career and your consequences. There's no need to defend your position, because ultimately, you'll decide your course of action. Use this time to genuinely listen and refine your approach.

Finally, conduct a "sound check" just like performers do before going live. Consider scheduling a follow-up session where you can practice your delivery and receive feedback on your tone, messaging, and potential impact before broadcasting your plan to those who matter.

The odds in corporate environments often favor those who already have power. Using strategic sounding boards effectively gives you a crucial edge in navigating these asymmetries. The right feedback at the right time doesn't just prevent catastrophic mistakes—it helps you spot opportunities others miss and approach them with precision others lack.

EXERCISE: THE SOUNDING BOARD AUDIT

1. List three people you typically consult for career advice.
2. For each person, identify potential biases that might influence their feedback (e.g., personal loyalty, hierarchical relationship, similar background).

3. Rate each on a scale of 1-10 for their willingness to challenge your thinking.

4. Identify one new potential sounding board who offers perspective you currently lack.

QUESTION TO REFLECT ON

When was the last time feedback from someone else fundamentally improved your approach to a challenge? What made you receptive to their input when you might have rejected similar feedback from others?

FIRST STEP

Before your next significant career decision, identify someone with relevant expertise who has no personal stake in your choice. Request 30 minutes of their time with a clear agenda and specific questions that invite critical rather than confirmatory feedback.

SHARING RISKS AND EXPANDING WITH EMPATHY PAYS DIVIDENDS

A personal reflection by

J. Phil Buchanan, CWS®, CFP®

EXECUTIVE CHAIRMAN OF THE BOARD, CANNON FINANCIAL INSTITUTE

"Being the boss" isn't anything like you imagine

WIN doesn't mean what you think

As a kid, I always thought "being the boss" was interchangeable with "leadership." Only when I got into roles that gave me responsibility for others did I come to understand the real requirements of leadership. It is not about feeling omnipotent and giving orders. Rather, it is about harnessing the collective energy of a group to move towards shared goals and aspirations. Harnessing that energy means driving most of the decisions down as far in the organization as possible. When individuals own the responsibility for their activities, they tend to make better decisions than those who wait to be told what to do.

The biggest lesson I learned is that as a leader, there will be tests and trials for which you have never been exposed or prepared to handle. It is in those instances that objectivity, lack of bias and a focus on W.I.N. (What's Important Now) are essential. During chaotic times, the success of your efforts to develop a top leadership team will be proven or disproven.

Fire up the way back machine: Summer 2007

The broad financial markets were humming along. I was Executive Vice President and Chief Operating Officer of Cannon Financial Institute, a leading professional development organization for the wealth management, trust, and family office space within financial services. Due to client demand, I had traveled over 200 nights in the prior twelve months. Clients were beginning to express concerns because real estate values were falling real estate values and they were seeing the impact on mortgage-backed securities.

August 19, 2007: Caught the truck, now what?

Due to health issues, our then CEO was stepping aside and I was moving into the CEO chair. It was like the Labrador puppy who chased 18-wheelers—I had finally caught the truck; now, what was I going to do?

Over the next few days, the surprise of the announcement passed, and the company rallied around me. I made a couple of tweaks to the leadership team to make sure we were a cohesive unit.

Fall of 2007: Licking our chops for the best year ever

For firms like ours, most engagements are multi-year relationships. In early fall of 2007, we inked a significant contract that would use significant capacity all the way through early fall of 2008. Added to already inked deals, 2008 was set to eclipse our best year ever.

2008: The financial plague afflicts us all

Enough has been written as to the timeline of 2008. Suffice it to say that all our clients were affected. As such, we were impacted. While most of our engagements went forward, it was clear that firms were battening the hatches for a long financial downturn.

I knew we were going to need to tighten our financial belt and intensify our business development efforts simultaneously. Cut spending and expand outreach. We came within a couple of percentage points of having a record year in 2008.

2009: Flex, tighten up, and keep breathing

The financial crisis was hitting hard. Entire segments of our business were almost dormant as client firms shrunk their expenditures. I tasked our leadership team with reimagining our structure in ways that supported high capability but created more financial flexibility. As a result, we exited a couple of business lines that were not core to our business. We realigned other segments under new leaders. We tightened the purse strings.

In the 15 years I had been with the firm, we had experienced a couple of challenging years, but nothing even close to the chaos of the financial crisis. Most of my weeks were 70-80 hours plus. Leading during times like those were not what I had envisioned, nor was I really prepared.

Cancel now for a profit or partner for potential gain?

During a weekend meeting the prior fall of 2008, we were reviewing our project progress reports. Several of our clients were asking to cancel their contracts for 2009. Doing so would trigger financial penalties, but their finance offices were okay with the penalties if it reduced the total obligations.

Agreeing to this would be profitable in the short run because we would be paid for *not* doing work. We would have almost no expenses to off-set the revenue. Yet, it would not be helpful to our clients, and it would negatively affect us over the long-term.

By risking being turned down, we had a turnaround

That Saturday afternoon, we decided to go back to the group of clients wishing to cancel and propose a restructuring of the agreements. While each differed slightly, the premise was simple. Pay only a portion of the contract fees in the current year—less than what would have been owed if they canceled—and pay the remaining fees over a two-year period. We knew there was significant risk as we had watched many firms fail, but we believed that by leaning into the challenges of our clients and working with them to push through, we would all benefit.

Not every firm agreed to our strategy, but most did. Many of these firms had gone through reductions in force and were stretched thin. Our involvement created more capacity for them. In many instances our consultants became adjunct professionals within their teams. Within several weeks, we were receiving requests to expand our involvement with many of the firms. In late 2009, our consultants were matching their work-levels from 2007.

The two biggest lessons I took from my early leadership days at Cannon are: 1. A strong balance sheet gives you options and emotional peace, and 2. Always look at a situation from the eyes of your clients—flexibility is always valued.

2013: When caring is business strategy

I believe in life-long learning. Professionally, I have grown exponentially from taking part in peer-group round tables and by serving on boards of other companies. In 2013, I had an exchange with the CFO of a company for which I was a board member. She presented a challenge to me along a list of names. These were over 15 women for whom the CFO wished to send to one of Cannon's programs. However, all these women were mothers of small children (some were single moms) and they did not have the flexibility to be gone for five nights to attend a program.

In fact, we had already introduced some remote programming, but not to the extent necessary to satisfy the CFO's goals. As a result of that conversation and with an eye on giving flexible options to prospective participants, we invested heavily in distance learning.

2017: Empathy leads to expansion

Four years after that conversation, Cannon's remote learning programs were the fastest growing segment of our company. By having multiple options available, we found we were extending our client base into firms we had never worked with prior. 2018 and 2019 saw continued growth in digital learning, but it still represented a minority of our work. Face to face programs would always be the top choice (or so we thought).

2020: A literal plague

January and February of 2020 were two of our best months ever. The economy was robust, and client demand was high. Having moved into the Executive Chairman role with Cannon a couple of years prior, I was primarily focused on client cultivation and development.

In March, I spoke at two conferences and then went on vacation for 9 days. We were all aware of the virus that originated from Wuhan, but did not comprehend what was about to be unleashed on the world. On day six of my vacation, I got a call from our president that three of our client firms had made the decision to send home all of their employees to work remotely. Based on this precedent, we both believed others would follow.

My family and I decided to change our return flights home. However, there were no other flights available. Those next two days brought more news of the spread of corona virus and likely lockdowns. My thoughts went to our firm and its projects for 2020. If a lock-down came, how would it impact our firm?

I arrived home from vacation on Friday evening. I knew things were different when my wife and I stopped at a grocery store. Shelves were empty—especially paper products. The next morning, our leadership team met in the parking lot of our office. We looked at the upcoming projects and analyzed the potential impact a lock-down would create. I smiled when one of our long-time leaders spoke up with "Looking at it from the client's point of view, wouldn't they want to use this time for professional development? Why can't we move everything on-line?" There was agreement among our team, but how would we pull it off?

From helping a few moms to being the go-to distance learning resource

The investment in digital learning that we made seven years earlier to create options for young mothers proved to be a key ingredient in allowing our company to excel during Covid. It took a lot of adjusting, but we had only two projects cancel in 2020. All others were conducted remotely. By having created flexibility for moms in 2013, we were able to provide flexibility for all our clients in 2020.

December 2024: Sustainable success comes when you consider others

I believe that all good leaders must have a perspective of flexibility. Consumers and clients want to consume your services on their terms, not yours. As I reflect, the Coca Cola company taught me this lesson when I was a kid. They made their product available on the consumer's terms. Eight ounces bottles or 2-liter bottles—the choice is yours. Do you want a Coke in a 12 ounce can or out of a soda fountain? Would you like a frozen Coke or a can of Coca Cola and Jack Daniels? The Coca Cola company lets you choose.

Full circle

Being "the boss" is not about command and control. It is about helping synergize the resources of the organization into a force that benefits clients, colleagues, and stakeholders. When done appropriately, you will note a couple of things: your colleagues stay with your firm longer than the averages and your firm becomes a "choice destination" for top talent within your industry.

ABOUT PHIL BUCHANAN

Phil Buchanan serves as the Executive Chairman of the Board for Cannon Financial Institute. As one of the most respected wealth management experts in the country, he has collaborated with major financial services firms across North America and their subsidiaries abroad, fulfilling roles as a speaker, trainer, consultant, and coach.

A prolific contributor to industry publications, delivers keynote addresses, and frequently engages with the media on wealth management topics, Phil also hosts four podcast series, focusing on leadership, entrepreneurship, and industry trends. Entrepreneurial by nature, he holds/has held positions as President of Argent Financial Group, non-executive Chairman of Laurus Holdings, and Board Member for LibertyFi, GreenHill Investment Reporting, the Association of Trust Organizations, and Lambda Housing.

Phil excels at simplifying complex concepts. Through his straightforward approach to practice management, he helps wealth management professionals advance their knowledge and skills, ultimately improving the client and prospect experience within advisory practices. He embodies the commitment to always provide clients with the best counsel and advice, regardless of how it might impact the advisor.

14

WHEN YOU GOTTA GO—
YOUR CAREER ESCAPE PLAN

The ancient samurai were known to meditate on their own deaths each morning. Strange practice? Perhaps. But there's profound wisdom in confronting the inevitable—not with dread, but with calm acceptance. The samurai who had already faced his mortality in meditation couldn't be paralyzed by fear in battle.

Your career deserves the same clear-eyed preparation.

Perhaps someone (maybe your parents or an older relative) is selling the comforting fiction that employment is permanent, that loyalty guarantees security, that your company "values" extend beyond quarterly profit margins. Maybe your boss or HR is selling you on employee-of-the-month plaques and anniversary milestone celebrations while conducting midnight meetings about which departments to downsize.

Here's an uncomfortable truth

Every career eventually faces its hurricane season, its wildfire warning, its tornado alert. The only question is whether you've prepared an escape route or will be caught scrambling when the winds shift.

I have always kept what I call a "career go-bag" packed and ready. Not just one, but several, strategically positioned where I need them most. And un-

169

like the metaphorical optimist who hopes for the best while ignoring gathering storm clouds, I've practiced grabbing them and moving—quickly, decisively, without the paralysis of surprise.

What's a career go-bag?

A career escape plan isn't just an updated resume in a folder. It's a comprehensive survival kit, meticulously assembled, that allows you to maintain not just your economic wellbeing but your dignity and psychological health when professional disaster strikes.

The difference between a career disaster and a career catastrophe isn't the event itself—it's your readiness. When the forest fires of corporate downsizing sweep through your company, prepared professionals calmly execute their escape plans while others stand open-mouthed, watching their professional lives go up in smoke.

The most successful people I know have been fired. The least successful people I know have also been fired. The difference wasn't in the termination—it was in what happened next. Those who thrived had already anticipated and prepared for the moment; those who collapsed hadn't accepted its inevitability.

The survival landscape

Before we pack our go-bag, let's survey the terrain. The corporate wilderness is changing faster than ever. Technology disrupts industries overnight. Algorithms replace human judgment. Companies merge, divest, pivot, and implode with dizzying speed.

In this environment, the concept of career loyalty has become as outdated as a fax machine. Your employment isn't a sacred covenant; it's a transaction that continues only as long as both parties perceive value. When that perception shifts, the relationship ends—often with little warning and less ceremony.

Companies will speak of "family" while designing your replacement. They'll celebrate your contributions on Friday and empty your desk by Monday. This isn't cynicism—it's the landscape. Navigating it requires clear vision, not comforting blindfolds.

Packing Your Career Go-Bag

Like any survival kit, your career go-bag must be tailored to your specific environment and needs. But certain elements are universal:

1. Financial Oxygen

The first item in your go-bag is financial breathing room—enough savings to sustain you without panicking. When career disaster strikes, nothing restricts your options more severely than immediate financial distress.

I've watched talented professionals accept degrading terms simply because they couldn't afford two months without income. I've seen brilliant minds surrender their negotiating leverage because the mortgage was due. Financial pressure turns career setbacks into career catastrophes.

Every bonus, raise, or unexpected windfall should be viewed as an opportunity to expand your financial runway. When a CEO once attempted to diminish one of my liquidity events by saying "it wasn't that much," I recognized the comment for what it was—an attempt to make me feel dependent rather than empowered. That "modest" sum purchased a Breckenridge condo with cash, expanding both my net worth and my freedom to make future career decisions without desperation.

Don't spend to impress others. Don't confuse possessions with security. The most valuable thing money buys isn't objects but options—the ability to wait for the right opportunity rather than accepting the first one.

I also have an uncomfortable relationship with debt. I don't like it. My advice is, whenever possible, avoid revolving credit card debt, car payments, or any other debt that has limited tax benefits. When it's possible, such as when you get a bonus, pay an extra mortgage payment or two to bring down principal loan amount.

2. Achievement Archives

Keep meticulous records of your professional accomplishments, stored where only you can access them. This isn't your company's performance review system; it's your personal catalog of value created.

Document three categories daily:

- **Completed tasks**: Note what you were assigned and how well you delivered on time, on goal, and on budget.

- **Initiative taken**: Record what you did beyond expectations—problems solved, processes improved, opportunities identified.
- **Connections made**: Log meaningful professional relationships established or deepened.

This archive serves multiple purposes. It provides ready material for resumes and interviews. It preserves your sense of professional identity during transitions. Most importantly, it prevents the common post-termination amnesia where shock temporarily erases your recollection of your own capabilities.

3. Professional Identity Documents

Your resume and LinkedIn profile are your professional passport and visa—the documents that allow you to cross borders between opportunities. Keep them current, accurate, and strategically aligned with where you want to go, not just where you've been. Get recommendations as soon as you sense someone is pleased to know you or appreciates your work, talent, or attitude.

Treat them these tools as living documents that evolve monthly, not emergency paperwork you hastily assemble after disaster strikes. The best time to update your professional narrative is when you're secure, confident, and clear-headed—not in the emotional aftermath of termination.

4. Network Navigation Tools

The most reliable emergency communication system isn't built in panic; it's maintained during peace. Your professional network should be nurtured consistently, not activated only in crisis.

Think of your network as a garden, not a vending machine. You don't plant seeds the day you want vegetables; you tend the soil year-round. Share insights, celebrate others' successes, offer help without expectation—these actions build relationship equity that provides support when you need it most.

The most pathetic sound in professional life is the voice of someone who hasn't been in touch for years suddenly calling with urgent need. Don't be that person.

5. Digital Cleansing Supplies

In primitive survival situations, contaminated water can kill you. In modern professional survival, contaminated digital presence can be equally lethal to opportunity.

Regularly inspect and sanitize your social media presence. Remove anything that projects unprofessionalism, controversy, or poor judgment. This isn't about censoring your authentic self; it's about recognizing that digital permanence requires thoughtful curation.

6. Adaptability Tools

The final elements in your go-bag are the tools that allow you to adapt to changing conditions—your skills, certifications, and knowledge. These should be continuously updated, expanded, and refined.

The professional who can only thrive in one specific environment is like a survival expert specialized in desert techniques suddenly dropped into the Arctic. Your ability to pivot, learn, and apply your capabilities in new contexts is what ultimately determines whether career disruption becomes disaster or opportunity.

Emotional preparedness: the hidden element

The most overlooked aspect of career survival isn't tangible—it's psychological readiness. When termination comes, the initial shock can trigger cognitive shutdown precisely when you need clear thinking most.

This is why emotional rehearsal matters. Periodically imagine receiving termination news. Visualize yourself responding with composure, executing your transition plan, and emerging stronger. This mental practice creates neural pathways that remain accessible even under stress.

The most resilient professionals I know don't just survive career transitions; they anticipate them. They cultivate what psychologists call "practical optimism"—the ability to face reality while maintaining confidence in their capacity to navigate it successfully.

The practice of readiness

Preparation without practice is merely wishful thinking. The career go-bag you haven't mentally rehearsed using is like emergency equipment with sealed instructions you'll be too panicked to read when disaster strikes.

Regularly conduct personal career emergency drills:

1. Review your achievement archives monthly.
2. Update your professional documents quarterly.

3. Nurture key network relationships monthly.
4. Assess your financial runway annually.
5. Enhance your adaptability skills continuously.

This isn't paranoia; it's preparation. It's the difference between the professional who stumbles disoriented through career transitions and the one who navigates them with purposeful calm.

The paradox of preparedness

Here's the ultimate irony: Those most prepared for career disaster often experience it least. Why? Because readiness creates confidence, confidence enables peak performance, and peak performance (sometimes) delays disaster.

But even more importantly, those prepared for worst-case scenarios make better decisions in all scenarios. They negotiate from strength rather than fear. They take calculated risks without existential dread. They speak truth to power without terror of consequences.

Preparation for career disaster doesn't make you paranoid—it makes you powerful.

EXERCISE: THE 90-DAY ESCAPE PLAN

Imagine your position was eliminated 90 days from today. Detail your specific action plan:

1. What immediate financial adjustments would you make?
2. Which three accomplishments would form the core of your professional narrative?
3. Which five professional connections would you activate first?
4. What skill gaps would most hinder your transition to your next opportunity?
5. Where would you focus your job search efforts?

QUESTION TO REFLECT ON

What invisible handcuffs are currently limiting your career options—financial dependencies, skill gaps, network weaknesses, or outdated professional narratives?

FIRST STEP

Identify one element of your career go-bag that's currently missing or outdated. Commit 30 minutes this week to addressing it, whether that's updating your LinkedIn profile, asking for recommendations, documenting recent accomplishments, or taking the first small step toward building your financial runway.

WHEN YOU REALLY GOTTA GO—
GRAB YOUR BAG

A personal reflection by

John Pierce

Which would you say is nuts? Expecting a disaster or ignoring the possibility? Call me nuts, but I aways have a go-bag ready to grab and go when a real-life disaster hits. In fact, I don't have just one go-bag, but several, packed in each place that I am likely to be. That means I've got a go-bag ready in my home in Florida, my vacation place in Colorado, and even in my truck. Depending on the amount of forewarning I get and the specific circumstances—I am ready to lift and load more than one go-bag.

No matter where I might be, I am never without a way to take care of myself if I need to escape, stay resilient, and recover when a crisis strikes.

What's a go-bag?

A go-bag is a carry-all that's packed with lifesaving supplies, plus what you need to survive for a while after a disaster hits. It's what I grab when the evacuation alarm goes off, an alert is issued, or I get a sense of imminent danger. Given where I live and travel, I've prepared my go-bags to flee a hurricane, avalanche, wildfire, or tornado.

I've packed them to get through the immediate crisis that lasts a few days and longer if there's no way to quickly get beyond the disaster area.

Given my outlook and experience, it's natural to take responsibility for myself and be prepared to help out others. That is part of having unshakable confidence—despite all odds.

Each of us will inevitably face natural disasters or other calamities. The difference between a disaster and a catastrophe may be your readiness. When you need to flee your home, be prepared so you avoid freaking out, running around in panic, or freezing with inaction. When disaster strikes or looms, it can feel overwhelming, frightening, threatening, and confusing.

I think the solution to all that chaos lies in the theory of Occom's Razor, where the simplest answer is usually the most elegant and correct approach. Simply put: Expect a disaster and plan to deal with it. Literally. Today you want to pack a go bag and practice lifting, loading, and packing it out to safety. If you live above the first floor, that means walking downstairs or throwing a rope ladder out a window and climbing down.

The most basic rule of survival

Never pack more than YOU can carry. So, either train for strength and endurance or expect to be cold, hungry, and vulnerable.

The second rule of survival: Identify all the exit routes because you can expect some to be blocked. If there's only one way out, then plan on getting out early so you don't get stuck or stampeded.

The third rule of survival: You may never need anything you've prepared to withstand or survive an emergency, but you'll always feel unshakable confidence that you can!

15

READING BETWEEN THE BOTTOM LINES: DECODING THE HIDDEN SIGNALS OF CHANGE

"**B**y the time it's obvious, it's too late." This simple truth separates those who merely survive change from those who capitalize on it. The world is filled with people who excel at adapting once disruption becomes unavoidable. But true masters of thriving against the odds aren't just reactive—they're prescient. They detect subtle shifts in the professional atmosphere long before storm warnings appear on everyone else's radar.

Remember Blockbuster? Probably not. In 2000, they had the opportunity to acquire Netflix for a mere $50 million. They passed, presumably because everything in their business still looked healthy on paper. By 2010, Blockbuster filed for bankruptcy while Netflix soared. The bottom line numbers hadn't yet revealed the seismic shift in consumer behavior or technology, but the signals were there for those willing to read between those lines.

The most vulnerable position in any ecosystem isn't being the smallest or weakest—it's being the last to recognize that the rules of survival have changed. The dinosaurs didn't die out because they lacked physical advantages; they perished because their environmental awareness hadn't evolved to match a rapidly changing world.

You, my friend, are not destined to be a corporate dinosaur—not if you develop the skill I call "future literacy."

179

The lost art of environmental scanning

Indigenous trackers can read an entire story from subtle disturbances in the environment that most people would walk right past—a bent blade of grass, a shifted pebble, an unusual silence. They're not using supernatural powers; they've simply trained their perception to detect what matters in their environment.

In your professional ecosystem, similar subtle indicators exist, but most people have trained themselves to ignore these signals in favor of more obvious metrics: quarterly reports, formal announcements, organizational charts. By the time change appears in these official channels, the real shift has typically been underway for months or even years.

The professional tracker—the person who thrives regardless of odds—maintains constant environmental awareness. They notice when the usual ambient noise of the workplace changes pitch. They detect when the pace of decision-making subtly accelerates or decelerates. They sense when conversations shift from long-term vision to short-term results.

These aren't vague intuitions; they're deliberate observations that, when compiled, reveal patterns invisible to those focused solely on their immediate tasks.

The three horizons of change detection

To develop your change detection capabilities, you must train yourself to simultaneously monitor three distinct horizons:

1. The micro horizon: Your immediate environment

This is the terrain directly around you—your team, department, and closest colleagues. Changes here often appear as subtle shifts in behavior rather than explicit statements.

Watch for:

- Increased frequency of closed-door meetings
- Changes in information flow—either unusual transparency or sudden opaqueness
- Shifts in how resources are allocated to projects
- Alterations in who gets invited to which meetings
- Changes in the tone and content of internal communications

A colleague of mine once noticed that the company's previously verbose CEO had suddenly become terse in his weekly emails. Others dismissed this as meaningless; she recognized it as the first signal that quarterly results had disappointed and belt-tightening was imminent. She adjusted her project proposals accordingly, focusing on cost-efficiency rather than expansion. When the official announcement came six weeks later, she was already positioned as part of the solution rather than part of the problem.

2. The meso horizon: Your industry and competitive landscape

This wider view encompasses your company's position relative to competitors, suppliers, and customers. It's about spotting shifts in the broader ecosystem before they directly impact your organization.

Watch for:

- Changes in how competitors describe their value proposition
- Shifts in what skills competitors are hiring for
- Alterations in customer expectations or behaviors
- New entrants approaching your industry from adjacent spaces
- Evolving regulatory attitudes or enforcement patterns

Consider how the rise of remote work began as a fringe benefit at tech companies before COVID-19 accelerated its adoption. Those who recognized this shift early—not just as a temporary pandemic response but as a fundamental rethinking of knowledge work—positioned themselves for new opportunities in virtual collaboration, remote team management, and distributed company culture.

3. The macro horizon: Societal and technological shifts

This is the broadest view—major currents in technology, demographics, politics, and social values that reshape entire industries over time.

Watch for:

- Demographic cohorts reaching new life stages
- Emerging technologies moving from novelty to utility
- Shifts in social values and expectations
- Changes in how people define success or well-being
- New forms of entertainment, connection, or information consumption

The professionals who recognized early that millennials valued experiences over possessions, sustainability over convenience, and mission over compensation didn't just adapt to these changes—they built entire careers anticipating and addressing them. Those looking at GenZ and GenAlpha are getting a grip on what changes are coming.

From signal detection to strategic action

Reading signals is only valuable if you translate those insights into advantageous positioning. Here's how to move from observation to action:

Step 1: Separate signal from noise

Not every change matters. The art of signal detection isn't just noticing everything—it's discerning which changes have potential significance. Ask yourself:

- Is this a genuine shift or a temporary fluctuation?
- Does this represent a directional change or merely an intensification of existing patterns?
- Is this isolated or part of a broader pattern across multiple domains?

Step 2: Project forward, not backward

Most people assess change by comparing it to the past. That's backward-looking analysis. Instead, use detected signals to project multiple potential futures:

- If this trend continues, what becomes possible or impossible in one year? In three years?
- What secondary effects might this primary change trigger?
- Who benefits and who becomes vulnerable if this shift accelerates?

Step 3: Position for optionality

Rather than betting everything on one projected future, position yourself to benefit regardless of which specific scenario unfolds:

- What skills will become valuable across multiple potential futures?
- Which relationships should you nurture now to enhance your adaptability later?
- What projects might serve as bridges between current and emerging realities?

Step 4: Create value from insight

The ultimate test of change detection isn't just avoiding harm—it's creating disproportionate value from your awareness:

- How can you help others navigate this emerging change?
- What solutions might address problems that haven't yet been widely recognized?
- How can you connect disparate insights into novel opportunities?

The courage to see what others don't

Here's what makes reading between the bottom lines so challenging: You'll often be right before you can prove you're right. You'll detect signals that others miss or dismiss. You'll see implications that seem implausible to colleagues still operating from yesterday's assumptions.

This requires a particular kind of courage—the willingness to trust your observations even when conventional wisdom contradicts them. Not the arrogance that dismisses alternative perspectives, but the quiet confidence to hold space for insights that haven't yet become consensus.

I once worked with a mid-level marketing manager who noticed subtle shifts in how young consumers discussed her company's products on social media—not outright criticism, but a gradual shift in tone that suggested the brand was losing cultural relevance. When she raised this in strategy meetings, her observations were dismissed as "anecdotal" and "not supported by the numbers."

Rather than backing down, she methodically documented these signals, connected them to broader generational shifts, and developed a small-scale experimental campaign addressing the emerging sentiment. Six months later, when sales reports finally reflected the change she'd detected early, her experiment had already produced promising results that the company could scale.

She wasn't promoted for spotting the problem early—organizations rarely reward those who see troubles coming. But she positioned herself as the person with solutions to a challenge everyone else was just beginning to recognize. Within a year, she was leading the brand's youth strategy.

The environmental scan as daily practice

Reading between the bottom lines isn't an occasional exercise—it's a daily practice of deliberate observation. Here's how to incorporate it into your routine:

1. **Diversify your information diet.** If you only read industry news, you'll miss broader social and technological shifts. If you only follow mainstream sources, you'll detect signals after they've become obvious.

2. **Create space for pattern recognition.** Your subconscious mind excels at connecting disparate observations, but only when given time to process. Build reflection periods into your schedule—even 15 minutes of unstructured thinking can yield surprising insights.

3. **Maintain a signal journal.** Document observations that trigger your attention, even if you're not immediately sure why. Review periodically to detect patterns emerging over time.

4. **Develop a network of diverse scouts.** Cultivate relationships with people whose perspective, experience, and information sources differ from yours. Exchange observations regularly.

5. **Talk to the edges, not just the center.** The most valuable signals often come from those at the periphery of systems—new employees, front-line workers, customers in emerging segments—rather than those at the comfortable center.

Thriving in the fog of uncertainty

The ultimate test of your change detection skills comes during periods of intense uncertainty—when economic indicators send mixed signals, when technological developments create both threat and opportunity, when social patterns undergo rapid evolution.

During these foggy periods, those with developed signal detection capabilities maintain clearer vision than their peers. Not because they can predict specific outcomes with certainty, but because they've trained themselves to recognize meaningful patterns amid confusion.

This clarity amid uncertainty is the foundation of unshakable confidence. Not the false confidence of believing you know exactly what will happen, but the grounded confidence of knowing you'll detect and interpret important shifts faster and more accurately than most.

When others panic in the face of unexpected change, you'll recognize the signals you've been tracking for months. When others freeze in indecision, you'll have already considered multiple scenarios and positioned yourself advantageously. When others react to yesterday's news, you'll be implementing tomorrow's solutions.

This isn't about having a crystal ball. It's about developing the observation skills, pattern recognition, and strategic thinking that allow you to thrive not despite uncertainty, but because of how much better you navigate it than most.

The ability to read between the bottom lines—to detect significant changes before they become obvious—isn't just another career skill. It's the meta-skill that ensures your relevance regardless of how dramatically the landscape transforms around you.

EXERCISE: PERSONAL SIGNAL DETECTION AUDIT

1. Identify three significant changes in your industry or profession over the past five years that caught most people by surprise.
2. For each change, retrospectively identify early signals that were visible at least a year before the change became obvious to everyone.
3. Reflect on which of these signals you personally detected early, which you missed until they became obvious, and what might have enhanced your awareness.
4. Create a personalized "watch list" of potential signals across all three horizons (micro, meso, and macro) that might indicate significant change relevant to your career in the next 2-3 years.

QUESTION TO REFLECT ON

What assumptions about your industry, profession, or career path do you currently hold with such certainty that you might miss contradictory signals challenging those assumptions?

FIRST STEP

Identify one information source outside your usual professional bubble that offers perspective from a different industry, demographic group, or worldview. Commit to exploring this source weekly for the next month, noting any observations that contradict or complement your existing understanding of trends affecting your career.

THE PAST IS NOT PREDICTIVE

A personal reflection by
John Pierce

I'm not sure that anyone in their correct mind would say "let's swim 2.4 miles, let's ride our bikes 112 miles, and then to finish the day... let's run a marathon! How did I get here? I was not an athlete in high school. I ran the mile slower than you can believe. I enjoyed high school but, sure didn't peak there. After working a few years for Merril Lynch, I figured something out.

I never had the "killer/competitive spirit" in high school or college. It started to germinate when I began working at Merrill. Now, that's not all positive. I was working more than 80 hours a week. With breakfast, lunch, and dinner, snacks, and drinks—the waistline started to expand, cholesterol went up, and the hair started to go.

Like most things in life, proficiency with something like health requires commitment and a workable plan. I needed to get in shape and lose some weight, even as I provided for my family. So, I started to jog, swim, and ride a bike. One step, stroke, and foot-pushing-the-pedal at a time. Did an Oly, did a half, and then started what became a lifestyle. It must be, because I have finished 13 full distance Ironman races.

Why did I continue? Peace. I found when I was doing solid Zone 2 training for years, I could wash away the day, the problems, and all the "to dos." Even while the Atlantic Ocean or Lake Erie smoked me in rollers, I found clarity, peace, and contentment. Did I expect that? NO. It is probably not reasonable— or even imaginable—to expect a result that evolves over years.

You become someone you don't expect when you do something different. In fact, you become someone no one expected. Yet, you can and you do. It's totally ok for everyone to think I have a loose wire as I choose to sweat through another workout while most folks are still asleep in a warm bed or vegging out in front of a screen.

No matter how anyone else was living their life, I had to find a way to empty myself out—to eliminate the constant and mind-numbing noise that surrounds us. Setting up these physical challenges delivered benefits well beyond just physical ones. I focus better when my cognitive gas tank is low. I think more coherently when I eliminate the constant noise—and get a break from the expectations that people try to put on me. For me, Man Versus Nature is a very good fight, because it cleanses my mind of any other stress. It may be something different for you.

Set your own goals—don't let work take everything you have. You need a "Man vs. Self" challenge to build your confidence. You need to see overtime you can set and master the challenges you choose for yourself. Then, be patient, watch yourself evolve.

And—occasionally choose to do something *for* yourself that you would have never considered in the past. I recently participated in a 6-hour event that I would call "Max Woo Woo." Let me explain the event. Then you decide if it this is Max Woo Woo or even farther out there.

The event was called "The Art of Surrender." It was led by Sara Beer at Higher Vibration in Jupiter, Florida. Not really a dude event and I had to make a hard, internal agreement with myself that I would not look at my Steelers game against the dreaded Ravens during workshop breaks. It's me and nine women, with two women facilitators. We started off by saying why we each were attending the event (I said peace and clarity in a time of severe turbulence).

We then had an "intention setting session" for the day over tea. I am wired to "do" and don't spend a lot of time writing down my intentions with woo woo wood being burned at the yoga studio. (The tea was nice, but it was not like the tequila shot I get at my barbershop.)

From there we experienced a Sound Bath, laying down on our yoga mats with eyes closed. (Sound Baths "bathe" you in sound with singing bowls.) Then we journaled as a bottle of calming essential oils were passed around—I had no clue what to do so I followed the participants and put the stuff on my wrists and wherever. Gotta say, it was calming.

Then we journaled. I've never journaled and didn't do too well—I wrote the questions down—"what am I attached to that I need to let go" and "what am I afraid of by surrendering?"

From there we had a gluten free lunch (and not a lot of meat) with more water and tea. Near the end, we did a "tapping" exercise, which apparently has something to do with circadian rhythms. Pretty out there—check it out.

We then experienced a gong bath—really.

Finally, we had a closing ceremony where each of us volunteered an experience we had during the program.

So, seriously woo woo, huh?

I'm completely thrilled that I did this. From the moment I signed up for it, the workshop activated my continuous learner gene—despite my extreme skepticism.

How far are you willing to go to get out of your comfort zone? It doesn't have to be full-on "Woo Woo." Just think about this challenge as Man Vs. Self— you against your entrenched, comfortable habits. The most formidable roadblock you have in life is you, when you are stuck in old patterns and habits. That's why you must intentionally challenge your beliefs and even your way of life.

Set up the conditions that help you see how you can evolve, get stronger, or excel at what you never thought you could do.

I never earned a varsity letter at St. France De Sales in Toledo, Ohio. Today, I am training for my 14th Iron Man competition. I am a living example of that financial products disclaimer and you can be, too. "Your past performance is not indicative of what you will do in the future."

While most of my friends would not believe I participated in a Sound Bath, a Gong Bath, journaled on a bunch of life questions, and lit some wacky incense, I'm thrilled I got out of my own way and my personal perceptions to do something way out of my typical box.

Don't be trapped by your past. Embrace it. Celebrate it. Mourn it a little. Then, figure out how to move forward in a different way, so you can a deeper, wide zone of confidence, clarity, peace, and mindfulness.

KNOWING YOURSELF IS THE BEGINNING OF ALL WISDOM.

—ARISTOTLE

PIERCE GUIDE FOR
SELECTING SOUNDING BOARDS

A high-quality sounding board helps you filter out emotional or irrelevant noise, guide your decision-making process, and assist in expanding your potential solutions. Choosing the wrong person to be your sounding board can lead to an echo chamber effect, where your ideas are simply reinforced without critical feedback or they introduce unnecessary conflict. A great choice fine tunes your judgement and actions. A poor choice might complicate or even poison your path.

Hence, selecting the person who possesses the right temperament, knowledge, and values as a sounding board is critical to your professional development. Whether you are selecting someone to help you sound out ideas about how to tackle a specific issue or as a long-term mentor, these questions include some you can ask directly and others you may reflect on.

Instructions

As you are thinking about specific issues or your career in general:

1. Identify three people who could function as a sounding board for you.
2. For each person, review the questions to select:
    a. Questions to reflect on so you can make a yes or no decision, and
    b. Questions you would want to ask directly. Feel free to put the questions in your own words or practice them, so they feel natural when you ask them.
3. Make your list and get ready for serious conversations that will lead to a great decision about the ideal sounding board for you.

PART 1: What to look for in a sounding board

When selecting someone to be your sounding board, whether for a particular situation or as a regular resource like a mentor, consider the following qualities and questions.

1. Specialized knowledge

❑ Does this person have expertise or experience relevant to the issue at hand?

2. Clear communication skills

❑ Do they articulate their thoughts in a way that "lands with you" or that you find easy to understand?

3. Objectivity

❑ Can they offer unbiased feedback, even when it may not align with your perspective?

4. Temperament

❑ Are they a good listener?
❑ Do they have an energy, buoyancy, or intellect that enlivens a discussion?
❑ Can they regulate emotions like anger, anxiety, or excitement and help you do the same?

5. Fairness and compassion

❑ Do they care about your goals?
❑ Are they able to offer constructive criticism without being too harsh or too lenient?

6. Values and philosophy

❑ Do they have a value system that aligns with yours, or one that you respect?
❑ Can they offer useful insights into handling obstacles, challenges, frustration, and pursuing ambition and happiness?
❑ Are they a role-model in the way they typically think and act?

PART 2: What to avoid in a sounding board

These questions are designed to help you gauge if a prospective sounding board might have tendencies that could cloud their judgment or prevent them from providing clear and useful feedback for you.

1. Bias or echo chamber effect

Avoid individuals who are too close to you emotionally or who always agree with you. Consider the following questions (whether you ask them directly or simply reflect on how you have observed the person acting in these situations).

- ❏ "How do you handle situations when you disagree with someone close to you?"
- ❏ "Can you give an example of a time when you disagreed with someone and how you communicated your thoughts?"
- ❏ "How comfortable are you providing feedback that goes against what you think I might want to hear?"
- ❏ "What steps do you take to ensure you are not just agreeing to avoid conflict?"

2. Oppositional attitude

Avoid "know-it-alls" and individuals who always play "devil's advocate," or seek their self-worth by making others wrong. To steer clear of these individuals, ask these questions.

- ❏ "How do you balance offering critical feedback without being overly contrarian?"
- ❏ "What is your approach to disagreeing with others—do you see it as a way to refine ideas or to highlight flaws?"
- ❏ "How do you ensure your advice is constructive rather than overly critical?"
- ❏ "Can you describe a time when you played the 'devil's advocate' and why you felt it was necessary?"

3. Self-interest

Watch out for people who might benefit from your decisions, as they may provide biased advice to suit their interests. To identify someone who may have a vested interest in your decisions and could provide biased advice, use these questions.

- ❑ "Do you see any way in which my decision could impact you or your work?"
- ❑ "How do you ensure you offer impartial advice, even if there's a personal stake involved?"
- ❑ "In the past, have you ever found yourself offering advice on a situation where you had something to gain? How did you handle it?"
- ❑ "How do you separate your personal interests from the guidance you provide to others?"

4. Lack of expertise

Don't choose someone simply because they are available or willing; they must add value through their knowledge or insight. To avoid picking someone without the necessary knowledge or experience, ask these questions.

- ❑ "Have you encountered a similar issue before? If so, how did you approach it?"
- ❑ "What's your background in [specific issue/topic]? How do you stay informed in this area?"
- ❑ "Do you think there are any aspects of this issue where you might not feel fully equipped to advise me or discuss the topic?"

5. Emotional involvement

A person who cannot separate their emotions from the issue may project their own feelings (especially negativity, anger, or toxic positivity) onto your situation, clouding their advice. To ensure someone is not overly emotional or projecting their feelings, consider these questions.

- ❑ "How do you manage your own emotions when giving advice to others?"
- ❑ "Can you think of a time when your emotions influenced the advice you gave? How did you correct for that?"
- ❑ "How do you ensure that your personal feelings don't affect your objectivity when offering feedback?"
- ❑ "When listening to others, how do you stay focused on their needs instead of projecting your own experiences onto the situation?"

PART 3: Qualifying questions for potential sounding boards

Use these questions to assess whether someone could be a good sounding board.

1. Specialized knowledge

❏ "What experience do you have in [specific area of concern]?"
❏ "Can you share an example of a time you navigated a situation like this?"

2. Clear communication skills

❏ "How do you usually approach giving feedback?"
❏ "What do you need from me to fully understand the issue?

3. Objectivity and fairness

❏ "How do you ensure your advice remains unbiased when advising others?"
❏ "Can you think of a time when you had to give feedback that didn't align with the person's perspective? How did you handle that?"

4. Temperament and listening skills

❏ "Can you describe your process for helping someone think through an emotional or challenging situation?"
❏ "How do you manage to separate your own feelings when offering advice?"

5. Compassion and goal-orientation

❏ "What motivates you to help others reach their goals?"
❏ "How do you balance providing tough feedback with being supportive?"

6. Values and philosophy

❏ "How do you approach challenges in your own life, and how does that shape the advice you give others?"
❏ "What are your core values when it comes to facing obstacles or frustration in your career or personal life?"
❏ "How do you think about ambition and job satisfaction? What roles do these play in your decision-making process?"
❏ "What philosophy guides your pursuit of happiness and balance in life?"
❏ "How do you handle setbacks or failures in your own ambitions?"

PART 4: Red flags to consider

After asking these questions, consider these additional signals that may cause you to avoid choosing someone as your sounding board.

- ❑ Do they tend to dominate conversations or make things about themselves?
- ❑ Have they given advice in the past that wasn't helpful or aligned with your needs?
- ❑ Do they seem disinterested or dismissive when you talk about complex situations?
- ❑ Are their values or philosophy in handling challenges radically different from your own in a way that might lead to incompatible advice?

Next steps

After choosing your questions and completing this worksheet for three people, you have started practicing for your conversations with prospective sounding boards. You may have already identified an excellent prospect or nixed someone who would not be a good candidate.

The next step is to initiate a conversation where you introduce the concept of needing a sounding board and ask your candidate if they would be willing to open themselves up to some questions about their background, values, and interests. If you get a yes, then you have permission to ask the questions you've chosen that are most relevant or important to you.

Remember, this relationship is meant to help you, so being selective will make all the difference in receiving useful, actionable feedback.

Extra credit

Consider whether YOU are a good candidate to be a sounding board by asking yourself these questions. Then, where you fall short, consider how you can listen or act more effectively so others can trust you for advice.

ASSESSMENT

PIERCE MODEL OF
REFLECTIVE ACCELERATION

Would you like to transform bad feelings and amplify the good ones, when you think about past interactions or events? Would you like to learn from what happened, gain mastery over your life, and feel more confident and powerful?

That's why I created the Pierce Model of Reflective Acceleration.

This framework is the fast path to capitalizing on the events in your life that might otherwise be underappreciated or unchallenged. It's like upcycling a battered, old table that you keep moving from house to house, and finally refinishing it to a polished, stylish, and desirable place to dine for the rest of your life.

Inspired reflection directs your brain to intentionally:

1. Sort out exactly what worked or didn't
2. Create choices that leverage your experience taking positive actions and eliminate ones that led to bad consequences
3. Rehearse your new choices and embed them in your brain so you're ready for the future
4. Repeat or scale your new approach to optimally create, handle, or otherwise overcome future problems and amplify the value of new opportunities

Inspired reflection dumps out emotions and gives you a clear head to logically restructure poor habits and reactive behaviors. You can use this process routinely to optimize your actions and eliminate unforced errors. This framework guides you to identify:

1. What needs to be adjusted, tweaked, avoided, or replaced
2. How or where you can use your new insights to accelerate your success

How does this reflection lead to accelerating positive and powerful actions? By "draining" the emotional thoughts and feelings from an interaction or event, you rapidly see the structure of what happened and find better approaches to use in the future. Oftentimes, what has clouded your decision-making is anger, jealousy, shame, disappointment, frustration, boredom, complacency, over-optimism, or pride. Inspired reflection focuses you on the facts not the feelings.

Learn by reflecting on what happened

By intentionally using your life as a learning laboratory, you ignite your power to be more present in every situation. Because you act as both the student and the teacher, this model boosts your self-compassion, confidence, and mastery plus you see more successful results. In effect, you are mentoring yourself. So, you've got 24/7/365 mentoring available, and it's free!

Inspired yet structured reflection accelerates your success because it intentionally breaks bad habits, rewards the positive ones, and helps you plan to be effective even in the most challenging situations.

It has another huge benefit for your well-being. By seeing your life as both 1) getting things done, and 2) training for peak performance, your brain learns to see what you previously feared were "bad things" as "great opportunities." That removes the sting from criticism or bad news. When something goes wrong, you feel your feelings, and then your brain frames it as, "Here's a lesson that I will use to build up a smarter, savvier, more successful me!"

When you reflect on your work and life as a way to train your brain, you are always progressing—even when on the surface it looks like you've made an error, gotten yourself into a conflict or jam, or even failed.

This framework puts the meat on the expression, "It's all good." Consider that as a credo. It's. All. Good.

Now let's get your brain ready to dive in with a reset exercise so you have clear, clean mindset to accelerate positive change.

Brain reset

There's three parts of a brain reset: breathing, bouncing, and clapping.

1. **Breathe**: We're about to do a 7 -1- 4 -7 breathing technique. Take a deep breath in through your nose for seven seconds. Hold it. Now quickly take in one more short breath. Then hold it for four seconds. Finally, let out the breath through your mouth for seven seconds while making a whoosh sound (if no one is listening).

2. **Bounce**: If you can, stand up and bounce on the balls of your feet for 10 seconds, breathing normally.

3. **Clap**: Clap your hands twice and slide them apart with the palms face down. You may have seen a card dealer in Vegas do this to signal a shift change so a new dealer can step in.

Okay! Now you're ready to embed the Pierce Model of Reflective Acceleration. You're about to optimize any success and make it a replicable practice that moves you quickly toward any financial or personal goal. The framework can work miracles on failure, transforming what went wrong into what will go right in the future.

THE PROCESS

Choose a conversation, meeting, presentation, phone call, event, experience, or other interaction that caused a shift in how you felt. Reflect on your feelings during the situation. Perhaps you started out calm and got angry. Perhaps you started out angry and started to feel ashamed. Perhaps you were optimistic and then became disappointed or frustrated. Maybe you started out disappointed but left feeling optimistic. Maybe you came in smug and left feeling shocked. If you're doing this for the first time, pick an interaction or event that resulted in your being disappointed, frustrated, irritated, or otherwise unhappy. It's easier to transform bad to good than it is to transform good to fantastic.

1 | **Describe the interaction or event.**

Who was involved?

Jot down exactly what happened, as if you were writing a screenplay for a movie. Describe the setting or environment, how the furniture was arranged or how the view looked, who spoke first, what happened next as best you can recall. Structure your description of what transpired using a step-by-step or play-by-play manner.

Now, circle, underline, or bold the significant, critical, or pivotal moments.

2 | How did you feel BEFORE the interaction or event?

What were you hoping would happen?

What were your fears or concerns about what could happen?

What bumps or obstacles did you anticipate?

How much planning or preparation were you able to do beforehand?

Did you have a chance to speak with anyone who helped you prepare?

3 | How did you feel DURING the interaction or event?

Review each step or critical moment and annotate them for what you were thinking or feeling at that time. You can use a range of feelings or thoughts, like "Wow, this is getting tense." Or "Hmm, they seem irritated, wonder if it is me or something else." Jot your observations down next to the steps or add new steps as you expand on your recollection of what happened.

By now, it may seem that you have are watching a movie, because you are seeing things vividly. Expect new insights to arise. At this point, your brain is working like a can opener, slightly opening the lid more and more as you go over what happened. Add in all your recollections as well as your new insights, putting a checkmark next to new reflections or underlining those that are most impactful.

As you look at your thoughts and feelings, evaluate whether they remained stable, steadily trended up or steadily trended down—or did they zig zag during the situation?

Make a note if you're having difficulty remembering exactly what was said or done—and make a guess as to why. Were you having a loud internal dialogue, did you have trouble paying attention, were you so aggravated that you did not do a better job of making your point, were you surprised at the response you got, or was there something else that got in the way of your being fully present?

4 | **How did you feel AFTER the interaction or event?**

Name the thoughts and feelings you had immediately after the interaction or event concluded.

Name the thoughts and feelings you have had since that time. Note if over time your thoughts and feelings have changed or increased or decreased. Have you felt regret, elation, vengeful, delight, hostility, satisfaction, sadness—or other emotions?

Now that you have clarified your recollection and processed your feelings, let's focus on learning, creating more choices, and being more intentional about creating success in the future.

5 | **What are three key learnings from this event or interaction?**

What seems to work best with other people on this type of issue or situation, or with this type of discussion, collaboration, or conflict?

What are two or three alternative ways you could have approached this interaction or event to get a better result?

When you think about what ignited the critical moments, what could you have done before, during, or afterwards to increase your effectiveness? For example, how could you have been better prepared or how could you have better prepared the other people in the situation? What words would you craft to be more impactful, more collaborative, or less confrontative?

6 | Now, revise your "screenplay."

Using your key learnings, consider the changes to improve your part of the script or the setting, or add some "scenes" before the main act. You might want to add more actors—or take some out.

Now, revise the screenplay based on those change—including your dialogue, tone (more enthusiastic, curious, supportive, strong, or neutral), setting, people, and the responses that would logically flow from your new "script."

Visualize a more positive and powerful result that is close to your ideal.

7 | Rehearse.

Use the brain reset again (7-1-4-7 breathing, bouncing, and clapping) to clear your mind so you can form a new "memory" that will become the framework for future interactions or events like this one.

Run the new scene in your mind (if you can, say it aloud).

How do you feel after this rehearsal?

What was the shift from your original feelings and thoughts to the ones you have after the rehearsal?

Thank yourself for being a great mentor and believing that you can do it—because you and your brain just created a brand new memory!!!

Rate yourself on this using this framework:

* I did it!

** I learned something!

*** I gained greater mastery!

**** I made progress toward a goal!

***** I feel more confident and powerful!

PART IV
SEEING THE LIGHT

*Act as if what you do makes
a difference. It does.*

—William James

16

THE JOURNEY FROM DARK TO DAYBREAK

When everything goes dark—when you've been passed over for promotion, when your project fails spectacularly, when layoffs hit your department, when the company reorganizes and suddenly your role is unrecognizable—your first instinct is survival.

That's natural. That's human. That's also no way to go about living for lasting success.

The journey from survival to thriving isn't just about enduring until external conditions improve. It's about learning to generate your own light even while navigating darkness. This is the essence of unshakable confidence—not the absence of difficulty, but the presence of something within you that transcends your circumstances.

Let me share a powerful story that illustrates this principle. François-Xavier Nguyên Văn Thuân was a Catholic cardinal who found himself imprisoned in North Vietnam for thirteen years. He could have merely survived—counting days, preserving energy, waiting passively for freedom. Instead, he chose to thrive by finding purpose even in confinement. "No, I will not spend time waiting," he declared to himself. "I will live the present moment and fill it with love."

Despite his severe constraints, he found ways to minister, secretly writing messages of hope on scraps of calendar paper, passing them to a child who delivered them to his village. For two months, he continued this covert ministry. Throughout his imprisonment, he even shared his faith with his guards.

This distinction—between waiting for victory and actively creating meaning regardless of circumstances—marks the difference between those who merely endure career setbacks and those who transform them into catalysts for growth.

The waiting trap

How many promising careers have been derailed by the waiting trap? Waiting for the "right" boss to notice your contributions. Waiting for that toxic colleague to leave. Waiting for market conditions to improve. Waiting for the "perfect time" to ask for what you deserve.

Waiting puts your power in someone else's hands.

I've mentored countless professionals who stayed in unfulfilling roles for years because they were waiting for some external circumstance to change. They were like mountain climbers who pitched a tent at the first sign of clouds, hoping the weather would clear—only to discover months later they'd been camping just a few hundred feet from the summit.

The truth is, the circumstances will never be perfect. The toxic colleague gets replaced by a different challenge. The supportive boss gets promoted away. The economic headwinds shift direction but rarely disappear entirely.

From passive to active

Seeing the light of day begins when you shift from passive waiting to active creation. This doesn't mean denying reality or pretending difficulties don't exist. It means recognizing that even in constrained circumstances, you retain the power to create, to serve, to learn, and to grow.

Remember Michael from our earlier discussion about pressure? When faced with an impossible deadline, he went into overdrive, feeling the pressure of the constraints. His colleague Sarah, facing identical pressure, saw opportunity amid the limitations. Same external reality, vastly different internal experience.

This shift begins with a simple but profound question: "Given these circumstances, what can I create today?"

Not next quarter. Not when conditions improve. Today.

The sunrise principle

Think about how a sunrise works. Darkness doesn't suddenly vanish in a flash. The transformation from night to day happens gradually, often imperceptibly at first. There's a moment—astronomers call it "civil twilight"—when the sun is still below the horizon but its light begins reflecting into the atmosphere. It's not yet day, but it's no longer completely night.

Career transitions follow this same pattern. The shift from career grief to greatness rarely happens in sudden, dramatic moments. It happens in small decisions that slowly accumulate into a new reality.

When James lost his executive role in a corporate restructuring, his first months were pure survival mode—networking frantically, taking meetings with anyone who would see him, sending resumes into the void. Six months in, with savings dwindling and no offers materializing, he faced a crucial decision: continue the increasingly desperate search or create something new from his circumstances.

He chose creation. Instead of more networking events and applications, he began offering free strategy sessions to startups in his industry. Not as a job-seeking tactic, but as a way to contribute value and have purpose while he figured out his next move. These sessions kept his skills sharp, expanded his perspective, and—most importantly—shifted his internal narrative from "unemployed executive" to "strategic advisor."

Within weeks, his energy transformed. The desperation disappeared from his voice. His insights deepened as he engaged with new business models and challenges. And yes, eventually one of those free consultations turned into a paid advisory role, which evolved into a C-suite position at an emerging company in his field.

The external reality—unemployment—hadn't changed immediately. But James had begun generating his own light rather than waiting for someone else to flip the switch. His civil twilight had begun.

Practical daybreak disciplines

The journey from surviving to thriving isn't some mystical transformation. It's built on practical disciplines that gradually shift your experience even when circumstances remain challenging:

1. **Build before you need it.** The best time to prepare for darkness is during daylight. Develop skills, relationships, and financial reserves while things are going well. This isn't pessimism; it's pragmatic confidence that recognizes both opportunity and challenge as inevitable parts of any career.

2. **Control your morning narrative.** The first thirty minutes after waking set the tone for your entire day. Will you immediately check work messages, letting external demands dictate your mental state? Or will you claim those minutes for reflection, gratitude, or strategic thinking—something that builds your internal resources before you begin responding to external pressures?

3. **Create something daily.** No matter how constrained your situation, identify one thing you can create each day—a thoughtful email to a colleague, a more efficient process, a moment of genuine connection with a client. Creation is fundamentally an act of power and agency because it is completely within your control.

4. **Protect your energy sources.** Identify what genuinely energizes you—not just what temporarily distracts or numbs. Is it time in nature? Engaging in your faith? Deep conversation? Physical exercise? Creative expression? These aren't luxuries; they're fuel sources for sustainable performance.

5. **Serve someone else.** Nothing breaks the spiral of self-absorption faster than genuine service. Find someone facing greater challenges and offer something of value—your time, expertise, or simply your full attention. This isn't just altruism; it's a powerful reminder of your capacity to make a difference regardless of circumstances.

The ultimate test

How do you know you've made the transition from surviving to thriving? Here's the test: when faced with difficulty, is your first response "Why is this happening to me?" or "What can I create from this?"

The first question—why me?—keeps you trapped in a victim mentality, waiting for something externally to rescue you. The second question—what can I create?—places you firmly in the driver's seat of your career and life.

This doesn't mean you won't experience disappointment, frustration, or even grief when facing setbacks. Those emotions are natural and appropriate. But they're not where you'll live permanently. They're places you'll visit before returning to the fundamental question of creation.

Beyond individual resilience

The most powerful demonstration of this transition comes when you begin helping others make the same journey. The problems that once threatened to consume you become the very experiences that make you valuable to others facing similar challenges.

I've watched professionals go from being devastated by job loss to becoming respected voices on career transition or leaders in their industry advising others. I've seen leaders transform health crises into platforms for teaching work-life integration. I've witnessed technical experts convert project failures into breakthrough approaches that advance their entire field.

This is the ultimate alchemy, transforming your darkest moments into light that illuminates paths for others.

Your daybreak decision

No one else can make this transition for you. The journey from surviving to thriving begins with a decision—not once, but daily, if not more often during the day—to generate light rather than simply curse the darkness.

This decision isn't about positive thinking or denying reality. It's about recognizing that between stimulus and response lies a space. In that space lives your freedom to choose. And in that choice lies your power to transform even the most challenging circumstances into catalysts for growth.

The cardinal's message to his village bears remembering: "Along the road you are traveling, you will encounter brambles, tigers, and other wild animals AND roses and beautiful views." The path contains both obstacles and rewards—your task is not to wait until the path is clear of all dangers, but to walk it with purpose, dignity, and awareness of the beauty that exists alongside the beasts.

So ask yourself: what are you waiting for? And more importantly—what could you create today while you're waiting?

EXERCISE: THE DAYBREAK INVENTORY

1. Identify a current challenging circumstance in your professional life where you find yourself in "waiting mode."
2. List three assets you still control despite these circumstances (skills, relationships, time, etc.).
3. Identify one specific creation you could undertake this week using these assets, regardless of whether external circumstances change.
4. Determine one energy source you'll protect during this challenging period.
5. Identify someone you could serve or support who faces even greater challenges.

QUESTION TO REFLECT ON

When in your past have you successfully transformed a period of "survival" into one of growth and creation? What internal resources did you draw upon that you might access again?

FIRST STEP

Choose one morning this week to establish a "creation before reaction" ritual. Spend the first 30 minutes of your day on something that builds your internal resources before checking messages or responding to external demands.

ROCKY MOUNTAIN WHY

A personal reflection by
John Pierce

On a day at my vacation house in Breckenridge, I needed to take a break and decided to hike up a hill there. I live near the base of peak 9 so I started to climb. As a flat lander—(I spend most of my time in June Beach, Florida)—it takes some time to adjust to the altitude. By now, I was doing ok without my heartrate spiking—just below optimal Zone 2. I climbed for a mile or so and then started down. This was late July, and the mountain snow melt was in full force. I spotted a gap in one of the streams. There was a dry patch in the middle. I had to use a rock and a downed tree branch to get to my destination. I sat on a branch, while the rushing water took multiple paths around me, as it flowed to the bottom of the hill that would eventually nourish millions of people.

I sat there for at least an hour just watching the water, as new circuitous paths established themselves. I was contemplating work and the next steps I could take in my life. In the calm of the rushing water, I realized "work" is not who we are. We need work to eat. We need work to pay our rent or mortgage. We need work to validate some parts of our past, maybe our education, or our parents' expectations, or our own self-imposed measures of success. Our work is not us; our work is merely part of us. Simply put: work should not mandate who you are.

As I stared at the stream and saw how many paths the water took as it flowed, I realized how much this reflected our lives. How many hidden and visible external forces, and internal factors, influence our lives to flow in so many different directions, I wondered.

On the left of the stream, a rock—that you could not see—was under the surface. It was a disruptor. The water rushed down and then encountered this hidden, underground obstacle. Some water went over it. Some water went to the right or the left. I have viewed most of my career as influenced by that big underground rock—The Disruptor—forcing it to go one way or another.

To my right, I saw this little trickle of water fighting to make it down the hill. The trickle needed to open space to be free, but it was hindered by sticks, rocks, moss, and pebbles. This stream was faced with—a Blockade. A lot of times, my blockade are my emotions. I shut down so that I don't cause more damage, hurt others, or feel sorry for myself. This is when I need to spend time in silence, in quiet, really turning off all the machines to contemplate the way forward and to unblock the stream.

Right down on one side, the water flowed freely, easy breezy, down the hill. So much of our lives are easy breezy and we don't really realize it—we don't appreciate it until there is an unanticipated obstacle or bad event. You lose a job. You lose your house. A friend dies suddenly. You lose a parent. Before you have your next "event" what can you do to recognize and appreciate the easy breezy times—the life stream that we could call Free Flow?

On that hike, I had forgotten my hat, so I had to move around a bit due to the bugs, and as I did, I moved a large stick and a rock that altered the stream to a new path. I altered the stream. I made it change. I altered the path. I chose a different route.

I was thinking that, throughout most of my 30-year work career, I was the rock under the water or just above the surface, altering the waters' path. It made me chuckle as I thought about a guy named Jack H. of Merrill Lynch. Jack was the grizzled old veteran that always raised his hand at national conferences to ask the difficult questions. We all know a "Jack" in our lives, and we appreciate them deeply because they care enough to ask the difficult questions, to press when the waters were not moving optimally, and to alter the location of the problematic rocks, without worrying about the personal cost to their job security or reputation.

You can see the C-Suite roll their eyes whenever Jack raised his hand. I became Jack at the end of my career, because if someone won't risk it—the firm just wades into a stream of indistinguishable mediocrity or worse. There will be a time in your career, likely not for a while, where you can risk being the one to alter the path.

As I sat between the streams on that day in Breckenridge, a kid stopped by to ask if I was "ok." It was a kind gesture. I was so deep in thought I believe he asked twice. I looked up and smiled and said, "all good." I had been lost in deep thought, untethered to my day-to-day reality. It dawned on me that I needed more of those disconnected moments so I could let my brain, emotions, and heart just "be." In fact, I realized, I was still recovering from an idiotic move that had eliminated my job and that event gave me the opportunity to reflect on what is important in life. For the first time in 30 years, I was surprised to discover that work didn't make my top five.

Here are some of the things I do that define me:

- Health and wellness—Getting in the exercise, nutrition, and sleep that I somehow neglected for years and probably cost me some clarity, calmness, and resilience I needed to succeed in the tough times at work.

- Family and friends—Putting the effort into showing up in relationships that otherwise easily slide out of consciousness when work consumes most waking minutes.

- Reading and learning—Committing to sit down every morning to read something meaningful and impactful, which includes philosophy, religion, and reflections of people who are smarter than I am.

- Spirituality and a practice of faith. Connecting to a higher power, which for me means going to mass as part of my faith, but includes reading poetry and enjoying nature, art, and mindfulness.

- Awareness and appreciation. Staying present for the beauty of little things in life like a message from a loved one and the delight of seeing a rainbow, a hummingbird, or a sudden downpour of rain or snow.

Here is what I urge you to think about, work on, and journal:

1. What is the Disruptor in your life today? Is it a positive factor or too dominating? How do you moderate its impact so you can open up alternatives, and feel more free flowing?

2. What is the Blockade in your life today? What can you do to mitigate its negativity or lessen its impact on your life?

3. If your life is free flowing today, how can you heighten your awareness of that and amplify the joy?

4. What three tangible steps can you take over the next 90-days to intentionally guide or alter the path of your life?

5. Outside of your career, what are the five things that define you? Even if you don't like your answers right now, it's all positive because your awareness can ignite new pathways.

17

CULTIVATING EVERYDAY TRANSCENDENCE: FINDING THE DIVINE IN THE DETAILS

I've watched thousands of professionals chase the elusive "meaningful work" like it's some rare Pokémon they'll only encounter after reaching level 50. They're waiting for the perfect role, the perfect company, the perfect assignment that will finally make Monday mornings mean personal fulfillment.

Let me save you decades of disappointment: you're looking for transcendence in all the wrong places.

That feeling you're chasing—purpose, meaning, spiritual alignment—isn't hiding in your next promotion or buried in some dream job description. It's right in front of you, camouflaged in ordinary moments you've trained yourself to ignore.

I discovered this truth during the most mundane moment imaginable: as a manager sitting in yet another meeting, watching a junior sales representative go through a pitch that looked like dozens I'd already seen. But something shifted when I noticed his hands trembling slightly as he clicked through slides. Instead of mentally checking out, I leaned in. Asked a question that showed I was paying attention. Watched his confidence grow as the presentation continued.

Nothing dramatic happened. The heavens didn't open. But in that small act of genuine attention, I found more meaning than in countless "important" meetings with executives.

Here's what nobody tells you about finding meaning at work: it's not about what you do, but how fully you show up for it.

The great divide that's killing your spirit

Most professionals have created a false dichotomy in their lives:

- Important work (that deserves full attention)
- Everything else (to be endured while thinking about something else)

This mental apartheid is costing you more than you know. It's not just robbing you of present joy—it's blinding you to opportunities, connections, and insights that could transform your career.

When you categorize 80% of your workday as "just getting through until the good part," you're practicing a particularly destructive form of spiritual absenteeism. You're physically present but mentally and emotionally checked out.

The irony? The transcendent moments you crave rarely announce themselves with fanfare. They sneak in through the back door of ordinary Tuesday afternoons, disguised as coincidences, unexpected connections, or moments of surprise.

But you'll miss them entirely if you're not paying attention.

Wisdom that works Monday through Friday

Every major spiritual tradition knows something modern professionals have forgotten: the sacred doesn't live in a separate realm from the ordinary—it's embedded within it.

Zen Buddhists have a saying: "Before enlightenment, chop wood, carry water. After enlightenment, chop wood, carry water." The transformation isn't in what you do, but in how you experience it.

Jewish tradition speaks of "kavanah"—the mindfulness and intention that transforms routine actions into sacred connections.

Christian monastics follow the principle that "to work is to pray," finding divine presence in mundane tasks performed with full attention.

These aren't abstract philosophical concepts. They're practical operating instructions for professionals drowning in meaningless busyness.

The ancients understood what we've forgotten: transcendence isn't something you achieve when circumstances align perfectly. It's available in any moment you bring your full, undivided attention to what's directly in front of you.

Microdoses of meaning

Stop waiting for the career equivalent of a spiritual lightning strike. Start collecting microdoses of meaning instead.

Microdoses are small, intentional moments of presence that, accumulated over time, create profound transformation. They don't require changing your job or your company—just your attention.

Here's how you start:

1. **The Three Details Practice**: Before your next meeting, commit to noticing three things you've never observed before. It might be a colleague's unique communication style, an unexpected connection between projects, or a new perspective on a familiar problem.

2. **The Sacred Pause**: Create a five-second transition ritual between activities. Before opening your email, entering a meeting room, or picking up the phone, take one deliberate breath. This microscopic margin between tasks prevents attention bleed and resets your presence.

3. **The Question Upgrade**: In your next five conversations, replace a standard question ("How's that project going?") with one that invites deeper connection ("What's been most surprising about that project so far?").

These practices seem trivially simple—and that's precisely the point. Transcendence doesn't require dramatic life changes or spiritual gymnastics. It requires showing up for the life you already have with fresh eyes.

Elevation through attention

How you do something matters more than what you do.

I've met janitors who approached their work with such presence and purpose that spending five minutes with them felt like a masterclass in dignity. And I've met C-suite executives so disconnected from the present moment that their seven-figure compensation couldn't buy them a single minute of genuine peace.

The difference wasn't their job description—it was the quality of attention they brought to their work. Their integrity about doing their job in its small and large ways is the difference.

This isn't about putting a spiritual spin on exploitation or pretending that toxic work environments are actually blessings in disguise. Some jobs and companies genuinely need to be left behind. But before you blame your role for your lack of meaning, examine how you're showing up for it.

Try this exercise: Choose one routine task you typically perform on autopilot—preparing for a client call, writing a report, even commuting to the office. Approach it as if you're doing it for the first time. Notice textures, sounds, sensations. Be curious about details you've filtered out through familiarity.

What shifts isn't the task itself, but your relationship to it. That shift is where transcendence begins.

The transcendent workplace

Celtic spirituality speaks of "thin places"—physical locations where the boundary between ordinary and extraordinary feels more permeable. Your workplace has thin places too, though they're not marked on any floor plan.

They might include:

- The moment of silence just after a difficult question is asked in a meeting
- The space between receiving feedback and formulating your response
- The brief connection when passing a colleague in the hallway
- The pause before sending an important email

These aren't just temporal spaces—they're opportunities for meaning to break through if you're awake enough to notice them.

The most powerful way to create more thin places—time when there is opportunity to truly connect? Bring your genuine presence to interactions. Create openings for others to do the same. You become a walking permission slip for authenticity in environments starved for it.

I watched a senior leader transform his team's culture not through reorganizations or process changes, but by becoming genuinely curious about people's lives. In one-on-ones, he'd ask, "What's giving you energy lately?" Then, he actually listened to the answer. In meetings, he'd notice when someone had something to say or more to say but wasn't speaking up. He'd express an interest in hearing their point of view.

Nothing revolutionary—just consistent, genuine attention. Within months, his team became the company's most innovative division, not because they worked harder, but because they had created an environment where people felt truly seen.

The discipline of wonder

Cynicism is intellectually lazy. It requires no imagination, no courage, and no vulnerability. It's the participation trophy of professional attitudes—available to anyone willing to point out what's wrong without contributing to what could be right.

Wonder, by contrast, is a discipline—a muscle strengthened through deliberate practice when everything around you encourages atrophy.

Practicing wonder doesn't mean ignoring problems or sugarcoating challenges. It means maintaining the ability to be surprised, to learn, to see familiar situations with fresh eyes.

The next time you find yourself thinking, "That's just how things are around here" or "Nothing ever changes," recognize it as a failure of imagination rather than an accurate assessment of reality.

Try this instead: become a student of the mundane. Choose one aspect of your work environment that you've stopped noticing—the weekly status meeting, the company's approach to client communication, the way decisions get made. Observe it with anthropological curiosity rather than habitual judgment.

What patterns emerge? What assumptions underlie the current approach? What would happen if one element changed?

This isn't just an interesting thought exercise—it's often the birth story of innovation. One person's ability to see extraordinary possibilities in ordinary circumstances has launched more successful careers and companies than any amount of the much-hyped disruptive technology.

When transcendence feels impossible

Let's be real. Some days, the idea of finding meaning in your spreadsheets or staff meetings feels about as likely as finding unicorns in the supply closet.

Everyone experiences spiritual dry spells—periods when work feels mechanical, relationships feel transactional, and transcendence feels like a concept from another dimension.

These seasons don't invalidate everything I've shared. They're part of the natural rhythm of growth. Even the most enlightened monks have days when chopping wood is just chopping wood.

The difference is what you do during these desert periods. Most professionals either redouble their efforts to manufacture meaning or give up entirely, concluding that transcendence is a luxury their particular job doesn't afford.

There's a third path: maintain the practices even when you don't feel the meaning.

Continue the sacred pause before meetings. Keep noticing new details. Ask questions that invite deeper connection. These aren't just techniques for accessing transcendence—they're disciplines that prepare the ground for its return.

Sometimes the most profound spiritual practice is simply showing up with integrity when inspiration has temporarily vacated the premises.

And if the dry spell persists? Borrow someone else's eyes. Find a colleague, mentor, or friend who sees meaning where you see only monotony. Not to adopt their perspective permanently, but to remember that your current perception isn't the only available reality.

From moments to movement

Isolated moments of transcendence are nice, but they're not enough to sustain a meaningful career. You need to connect these dots into a coherent narrative—a story about work that's bigger than titles, compensation, or achievement.

Consider keeping a "transcendence inventory"—a simple record of moments when you experienced unexpected meaning, connection, or insight at work. Review it regularly to identify patterns. Under what circumstances do these moments tend to occur? What was present in you that allowed you to notice them?

These patterns become your personal roadmap to meaning—far more useful than generic career advice or only finding inspiration from others' journeys.

Then, design your environment to support awareness. Create what behavioral scientists call "triggers"—small environmental cues that remind you to pay attention. It might be a particular object on your desk, a recurring calendar reminder, or a ritual you perform at transition points in your day. For example, a friend of mine taps her thumb and forefinger together and gets in a breath to clear her mind between tasks.

The goal isn't to manufacture transcendence on demand—that's not how it works. The goal is to create conditions where you're more likely to notice it when it appears.

Remember, meaning isn't something you achieve once and possess forever after. It's a currency that must be continually renewed through attention and presence. The question isn't "Have I found meaningful work?" but "Am I bringing meaning to this moment of work?"

The choice before you

You're standing at a crossroads right now. Not the dramatic kind with lightning in the background and ominous music playing. The ordinary kind that appears countless times throughout your workday.

One path leads toward more of the same—going through the motions while waiting for some future circumstance to deliver the meaning you crave.

The other path leads toward the transcendence that's been hiding in plain sight all along—available not someday, but today, in the very next interaction, task, or meeting you encounter.

The path you choose won't be determined by what you read here, but by what you do in the next five minutes after you finish reading.

Will you immediately check your phone, respond to that notification, or jump to the next item on your to-do list? Or will you pause, even for a moment, to notice where you are, who you're with, and what opportunity for meaning might be present in this ordinary moment?

The divine isn't hiding in the details of some future, better version of your career. It's in the details of the workday you're living right now—if only you have eyes to see it.

In your personal life, use the same path to transcending the concerns you face in your life or with those you love. As I write this, I am reflecting on three difficult conversations I had this morning—an unfortunate trifecta of dear friends all struggling with medical problems that may be unsolvable. After the calls and a swim in ocean, I just stopped. I stood on the sand, closed my eyes, and shut out the people and all the other distractions. Just listening to the ocean and the sound of my own breath helped me restore my sense of inner peace and inner strength.

EXERCISE: THE DIVINE DETAILS INVENTORY

1. List three routine activities in your workday that you typically perform on autopilot—activities where you're physically present but mentally elsewhere.
2. For each activity, identify what specifically you're missing when you're not fully present. Is it opportunities for connection? Creative insights? Chances to demonstrate your values?
3. Create a simple "transcendence trigger"—a physical cue or brief ritual that reminds you to pay attention during these activities. It might be touching a certain object, taking a specific breath, or reciting a personal mantra.
4. Commit to one week of bringing extraordinary attention to these ordinary activities. Document any insights, connections, or moments of meaning that emerge.

QUESTION TO REFLECT ON

When was the last time you experienced a moment of unexpected meaning, connection, or insight during a routine workday? What made that moment different from others? What would change if you could bring that same quality of presence to more moments of your professional life?

FIRST STEP

Choose one conversation you'll have tomorrow—a team meeting, a one-on-one with a colleague, a client call. Commit to approaching it with extraordinary attention. Notice three details about the interaction that you would typically miss. After the conversation, ask yourself: What did I discover when I was fully present that I might have missed otherwise?

SIMPLY PARIS

A personal reflection by
John Pierce

One of my most favorite places on earth is Paris.

I took my daughter there when she was 10. We went for a week on a tour ... the PBS Rick Steves tour. He really is America's leading expert on European travel. That tour was amazing, and I've been back five or six times since then. Here's why.

I think Paris is so simple and so lovely and just so completely different from my experiences in any other place on the planet. Now, what's funny about this is a dear friend of mine was like ... you're out of your mind. She said, "Paris is one of the most sophisticated places on the planet. For example, it is a mecca of food."

In response, my take on Paris is this. It is a mecca of commerce and finance and art and history and all. That's true. But I see Paris from a different perspective. I love getting up in the morning and having a cappuccino, having an espresso sitting down, not walking with it—like we do in the US.

I like going to market and buying my food daily. Fresh food, no preservatives. I like drinking the wine with no sulfites and no hangovers.

The metro is a simple way to get around.

The reason I bring up these dueling ideas about one place—is that you can have a different perspective on work, on location, on many things in your lives. Your take can be diametrically opposed to what other people think. It's important to have your perspective, and then it's important to listen to other people's perspectives as well. That's how you grow. That's how you become better.

As for the city of lights. I will always enjoy sitting on the lawn when the Eiffel Tower is lit up at night. I'll always enjoy that baguette in my backpack and the simple wine when I'm having some food at lunch.

Point is: Enjoy your perspective but also embrace other people's perspectives when you can. Let people be different from you—and at the same maintain your own unique perspective, even when "commonly held" beliefs don't fit your view of the world. I have often found that when I consider the perspective of another person, one that is completely different from mine, I can grow and learn from them. I may not adopt their perspective, but it allows me to pause longer and think deeper before opening my mouth. That openness is a form of personal growth that benefits each of us.

That's the only way to go through life. It's a simple philosophy and it is simply the best way to go through life.

18

CONNECTING TO CALM WITH FAITH

In a world of relentless pressure, noise, and expectations, finding calm isn't just a luxury- it's a necessity for survival and success. Most of us recognize this intuitively. When it's been too long since we've had a moment of stillness, we feel restless, depleted, exhausted, and out of sorts. We see it in our decisions when impulse and emotion win over clarity and deliberation. We experience it in our relationships when tension and explosion replace connection and compassion. Spinning out from one moment to the next, it's easy to spiral down into physical, cognitive, and emotional depletion.

When you're in the throes of corporate life—the endless meetings, quarterly targets, strategic pivots, and organizational politics—calm easily becomes the first casualty. The irony is stark: the more we need that stillness, the more elusive it becomes. Rarely does someone at work or even at home say, "I think you need some time to restore yourself." And yet, you're not going to last if you are always producing, grinding, and stomping out fires.

The search for stillness

The concept of "faith" can be a difficult topic to discuss. Most people have faith in something—faith in yourself, faith in a process, faith in your family or friends. But the "Big F" Faith—belief in a higher power or spirituality—is something many people don't openly discuss. They even actively hide it for fear of rejection, judgment, or misunderstanding.

I view my Faith as I view the personal, raw reflections shared throughout this book—as an extraordinary experience that requires stepping outside comfort zones to acknowledge its true power. But I approach it in my own unconventional way.

For more than 40 years, I've sought places of calm where I can decompress, clear my head, and turn off the chaos that life inevitably brings. I've found two geographical sanctuaries where calm comes naturally:

- Walking the uninhabited southern stretch of Juno Beach, where the sand slides between my toes and waves lap at my feet is a natural sanctuary. Instead of following crowds north through what I jokingly call "thongville," I head south to observe brilliant clouds at sunrise, sunset, or as storms roll in from the Atlantic. When I head into the ocean for open water swimming, I feel nature's raw power as huge rollers toss me about—and I discover the absolute calmness and beauty that exists just beneath the angry surface when I dive below a crashing wave.
- Hiking the mountains in Breckenridge, Colorado, where I can wander for hours seeing only a handful of people is another natural sanctuary I revel in. There, I marvel at the trees, feel the wind shifts, absorb nature's sounds, and appreciate the purity of snowmelt streams or the satisfying crunch of snowshoes on fresh, unmarked snow.

These natural experiences where I find calm reveal something profound—there exists something much bigger and more amazing than myself or any human being. Through corporate climbs, career setbacks, personal failures, and the general grind we call work and life, these moments of natural stillness have consistently whispered that there is more than just our brief lifespan. When I achieve that natural stillness under the water, walking the beach, or climbing the hill, it just shouts out to me that there is more than just our 90-year lifespan.

The sanctuary of ritual

The other place I find peace, calm, and quiet is at daily mass. This hasn't been a lifelong habit, but one I've cultivated over years when I'm home. It's probably no surprise that I prefer weekday services to weekend ones—I'd rather avoid the loud music, lengthy homilies, and crowds with unsilenced cellphones. (Did lightning just strike for my honesty?)

This practice began during my Merrill Lynch days, with 7 a.m. mass before driving to downtown Cincinnati. At Stifel in St. Louis, I'd break away for noon mass when it was possible. In Breckenridge, Tuesday and Thursday 8 a.m. masses provide structure; in Palm Beach, St. Patrick's 8:30 a.m. mass offers connection with my parents who winter near my home there.

Like my experiences in nature, mass brings a different type of calm—a stillness where I can sit in solitude and embrace quiet reflection. In the busiest periods of my career, these moments weren't luxury; they were necessity.

The rhythm of renewal

I've learned we humans don't have on/off switches—at least I don't. We grind. We produce. We care for families. We fill our lives with activities like children who stuff marbles in jars until they overflow, yet it's never enough. That's what you do until you learn that you must find time to stop. You must find time for calm.

Every day you have the chance to find a moment to affirm that the past is finished—you can only learn from it, not change it. Every day you can take a moment to recognize that the future is unknown—you can't afford to expend mental and emotional energy worrying about "what ifs." You and I can take each day anew, and because I am mindful that my choices are the part of life that I can control, I consistently search for calm.

That calm comes from geographical places and has its foundation in "Big F" Faith, not just the "little f" faith in myself. The places where I find calm couldn't exist without something greater, because no human could ever explain, replicate, or create a roaring ocean, massive snowfall, or the peace I experience during mass.

Faith as a leadership foundation

In leadership positions, I've found this foundation of Faith particularly valuable during crisis moments—when markets crashed, when key team members unexpectedly departed, when strategies failed despite perfect execution, and when someone dear to me died suddenly. These moments test not just your skills but your core.

During the 2008 financial crisis, as colleagues panicked about plummeting portfolios and vanishing bonuses, my morning ritual of mass provided perspective that money and markets, while important, weren't ultimate. This wasn't fatalism or disengagement—quite the opposite. It freed me to make clearer decisions unclouded by fear.

When facing a particularly difficult termination conversation with a once-promising executive, the calm I'd cultivated through Faith allowed me to approach the situation with both necessary firmness and genuine compassion. I could separate the person's intrinsic worth from their performance issues.

And in moments of personal failure—missing targets, misjudging situations, damaging relationships through thoughtless actions—Faith provided both accountability and forgiveness. I could face my mistakes squarely without being crushed by them.

Faith beyond crisis

What you cultivate, grows. What you invest in, compounds. Do not think that an emergency will make the resources you need suddenly appear.

Faith isn't something you just pull out when bad things happen. In fact, if you don't have Faith when your world crumbles, having a conversion moment will leave you disappointed—trust me, I know from personal experience.

My daily encounters with nature reaffirm my belief in Faith. My dedication to a regular practice in a faith-based community builds my relationship with a higher power.

While I would be remiss to not share this with you now—as we look at all the roads that lead to unshakable confidence—I never evangelize or shout from rooftops. I trust that how I live, how I course-correct, how I treat and recognize people, and how I listen demonstrates my Big F Faith more eloquently than words. Too many people wander in darkness, in mist, in cold isolation without guidance. Helping others turn off noise, find calm, and understand its source—in my case, Faith in something gigantically bigger than myself—becomes a step toward a more caring and loving workplace and society.

It starts with each of us taking a step back, finding our calm, and recognizing that Faith derives from something beyond any human being—something larger that we can't fully comprehend. Free Will allows for both good and bad choices. It takes our God-given Free Will to explore building a foundation based on Faith that produces the calm each of us seeks—and needs—to live and lead with unshakable confidence.

Find your own sanctuary

While my path to calm comes through Catholic faith and living in natural settings, yours may differ entirely. The principle remains: leaders who intentionally practice inner calm so it is a bedrock of their lives, make better decisions under pressure.

Consider:

- Where do you feel most at peace?
- What practice helps you step outside the noise of daily demands?
- How might you incorporate moments of stillness into your leadership routine?
- When facing your most challenging leadership moments, what grounds you?

The strongest leaders I've known—regardless of their specific beliefs—maintain some practice that connects them to something larger than quarterly results or organizational politics. Whether through formal religious observance, meditation, time in nature, or creative expression, they find ways to regularly quiet the noise.

In a business culture that often celebrates constant connection and relentless hustle, intentionally disconnecting becomes a revolutionary act of leadership—and perhaps the most important one for maintaining the unshakable confidence this journey requires.

EXERCISE: THE SANCTUARY MAP

1. Identify three places where you naturally feel calm and centered. These might be physical locations (a park, a room in your home, a coffee shop) or activities (running, playing music, cooking).
2. For each place or activity, note what specifically creates the feeling of calm or connection (solitude, sensory engagement, rhythm, beauty, etc.).
3. Reflect on whether these elements connect you to something larger than yourself—whether that's nature, community, creativity, or spirituality.
4. Create a "sanctuary schedule"—specific times in your weekly calendar dedicated to visiting these places or engaging in these activities.
5. After two weeks of following this schedule, note any changes in your decision-making, relationships, or overall sense of confidence.

QUESTION TO REFLECT ON

When was the last time you felt truly calm in the midst of professional chaos? What created that calm, and how might you intentionally cultivate more of those moments, especially when you need them most?

FIRST STEP

Choose one ten-minute period tomorrow—perhaps before an important meeting, after a difficult conversation, or during a typically stressful part of your day—and dedicate it to finding calm through whatever practice resonates with you. This might be stepping outside to observe nature, sitting in silence, practicing conscious breathing, or connecting with your faith tradition. Notice how this brief sanctuary affects your perspective and approach to the balance of your day.

BEYOND LATTES AND THE LOTUS POSE: DISCOVERING YOUR THIRD PLACE

A personal reflection by

Chantalle Couba

TRANSFORMATIONAL EXECUTIVE COACH

Our lives typically revolve around two primary spaces: our homes and our workplaces. A third space may ignite newfound meaning to build your future.

When individuals describe where their lives are centered, they typically describe the places where they reside and work. Yet there exists another vital dimension that sociologist Ray Oldenburg calls the "third place." This is neutral ground where people can gather and interact freely, unburdened by their usual roles and responsibilities. Think of a third place as a physical location where you are unburdened by any family or work roles, like the freedom found walking in a nearby park, walking a beloved dog, being greeted at a favorite coffee shop or yoga studio.

The space for coaching

Executive coaching creates this kind of space, though in a figurative way. Like the community spaces Oldenburg studied, coaching provides neutral territory—neither the client's domain nor mine—where unedited dialogue can occur. It operates beyond workplace constructs while maintaining enough structure to support meaningful growth. Here, titles and roles are suspended to create the space to reflect, and the true expectation is presence.

In my observation, gaining access to the coaching space remained elusive, its entrance guarded by traditional human resources players who treated coaching like a bespoke garment, reserved for those already granted access to leadership responsibilities and tables. Women, minorities, and those not labeled as "high-potential" found themselves on the outside, watching others receive this gift of space. This selective access overlooked a fundamental truth: leadership potential exists everywhere—it simply needs the right conditions to seed and grow.

My journey into coaching began with this recognition: the transformative power of having a space that belongs neither to the professional stage nor the domestic zone. Think of it as stepping into a the proverbial phonebooth, where instead of preparing to transform into a superhero, we draw the curtains or today, turn off the virtual camera, allowing new thoughts to emerge from the change in location and pace.

Safe and truly free to explore

In this narrowly held space, something extraordinary may occur. Dr. Monica McGrath, in her insightful book "Learning From Business Leaders: A Coaching Memoir" (2024), observes that leaders often describe feeling trapped—constrained by the very roles and responsibilities that define their success. Yet in the coaching space, like standing at a favorite shoreline or finding solitude in a garden, these same leaders discover a different lens through which to view their world. What surfaces instead is psychological safety and freedom—a rare opportunity to examine challenges not as fires requiring immediate extinguishing, but as interesting puzzles worthy of careful contemplation.

The coaching space allows for self-reflection and human connection. Here's the paradox: while many of us naturally create these spaces for others, we rarely grant ourselves permission to drop anchor. We become so skilled at performing our various roles, that we forget how to step off the stage.

Through my own development journey, I discovered the profound relief of having designated time and space where I could explore and reflect upon my leadership voice absent of the need to assuage others. This experience was restorative. It wasn't just about professional growth; it was about rediscovering parts of myself that had been muted by the constant buzz of responsibility and at times, chaos.

Now, as a coach, I have the privilege of creating these spaces for others. When a client enters our coaching environment, whether virtual or physical, they step into a mental third space sanctuary, free from the orbital pull of both home and office. Here, they don't need to be the unwavering leader, the ever-present partner, or the engaged parent. They can simply be —questioning, uncertain, hopeful, afraid—embracing all the complex self that we often feel compelled to wash over in other areas of our lives.

Take risks and share vulnerabilities

The impact of this psychological safety reveals itself in remarkable ways. Researcher Amy Edmondson defines psychological safety as "a belief that one will not be punished or humiliated for speaking up with ideas, questions, concerns, or mistakes." In the coaching space, this safety becomes transformative. As McGrath notes, when leaders find this freedom from feeling trapped, they begin taking the kind of interpersonal risks Edmondson identifies as crucial for learning and growth—sharing vulnerabilities, admitting uncertainties, and exploring new possibilities without fear of judgment.

I've witnessed this evolution countless times. Leaders who initially guard their challenges begin to explore their frustrations openly. These shifts occur not because coaching provides a map with all the answers, but because it creates what Edmondson calls a "psychologically safe container"—a space where taking risks becomes possible, even inviting.

What energizes me most about coaching is its power to cultivate the conditions Edmondson describes as essential for psychological safety: setting clear boundaries, inviting participation, and responding productively to vulnerability. This safety, when properly nurtured, ripples far beyond individual coaching sessions into broader organizational learning. My work as an organizational improvement coach and practitioner has proved integrated workplaces don't happen by accident—they require intentional effort and commitment. The same holds true for psychological safety in organizational learning.

Safe space transforms performance

In the coaching space, we create room to realize what's possible when psychological safety meets organizational support. Leaders learn to recognize and challenge their unconscious categorizations and develop new mental models for leadership that embrace both vulnerability and strength. Most importantly, they experience firsthand how psychological safety transforms performance—a lesson they often carry back to their teams and organizations.

When leaders experience this kind of safety in coaching, they become more likely to create it for others. I've watched clients move from guarding their own uncertainties to actively creating spaces where their team members can speak up, take risks, and contribute fully. This multiplication effect can turn individual coaching insights into organizational transformation. When people believe their organization genuinely cares about their growth and well-being, they become more willing to take the interpersonal risks necessary for innovation and learning, formally known as perceived organizational support.

This understanding has deepened my appreciation for how coaching can serve as a readier for organizational change. When we create these safe spaces for leaders, we're not just facilitating individual growth—we're seeding the ground for what Edmondson calls "teaming intelligence" and what I describe as true workplace integration. Leaders who experience psychological safety in coaching often become its most effective advocates, understanding how this safety enables the kind of diverse, innovative thinking that drives organizational success.

The journey from seeking coaching to becoming a coach has taught me that true growth requires both physical and psychological space—room to breathe, to think, to question, and ultimately to transform. By creating and protecting these neutral grounds, I strive to contribute to a more humane and inclusive professional landscape, where everyone has access to the transformative power of purposeful reflection.

In this space between home and work, between who we are and who we're becoming, we find the freedom to explore, to grow, and to reimagine what's possible.

ABOUT CHANTALLE COUBA

Chantalle Couba is a transformational executive coach and organizational strategist with over 15 years of experience driving sustainable change across premier institutions. Her doctoral research on "Understanding Professional Resource Exchange Among Women in Leadership Positions" grounds her evidence-based approach to leadership development and organizational transformation.

As a trusted advisor to C-suite executives and senior leaders in both public and private institutions, Chantalle specializes in creating psychologically safe spaces that enable authentic leadership and foster inclusive cultures. Her global perspective is enriched by her selection as an Eisenhower Fellow and her international work spanning social finance initiatives in Haiti and inclusion research in the Netherlands and South Africa.

She frequently contributes to advancing industry dialogue through keynote presentations and expert panel facilitation at leading conferences, while sharing insights on organizational transformation and strategic partnerships through broadcast and print media.

As a Distinguished Lecturer at premier research universities, she bridges cutting-edge research with practical application. Chantalle holds a doctorate in Adult Education from the University of Pennsylvania, a master's in Instructional Design and a bachelor's in English literature from Florida State University.

Connect with Chantalle at leadersgenerate@outlook.com

19

WHEN YOUR PERSONAL WORLD COLLAPSES: FINDING REFUGE IN YOUR PROFESSIONAL LIFE

It happens to everyone eventually. The call in the middle of the night about a loved one's health emergency. The conversation that ends a relationship. The discovery of a friend's betrayal. The accident that changes everything in an instant.

Life doesn't politely wait for your career to reach a convenient stopping point before it throws you into crisis. And somehow, through it all, you're still expected to show up to your 9 AM meeting, complete your project deliverables, and respond to that flood of emails with your usual efficiency.

I've watched many promising young professionals navigate this impossible terrain—when their personal worlds collapsed but their work responsibilities couldn't be put on hold. Some struggled to maintain even basic functioning, while others found unexpected strength. The difference wasn't in the severity of their crises, but in how they approached the dual challenge of maintaining professional stability while facing personal turmoil.

Let me share what I've learned from observing these journeys up close.

The sanctuary of structure

When personal crisis hits, your first instinct might be to call in sick indefinitely. To put your career on hold while you deal with the "real emergency." This instinct, while understandable, is often misguided.

Here's why: during times of personal chaos, the structure of work can provide a critical sanctuary. The rhythm of meetings, deadlines, and familiar tasks creates a framework that holds you together when everything else seems to be falling apart.

I've seen this repeatedly with younger colleagues facing devastating personal circumstances. One associate maintained a modified work schedule throughout a parent's serious illness—not because he was insensitive or career-obsessed, but because those hours provided a temporary respite from the consuming uncertainty at home. In the hospital waiting room, he could control nothing. But for those few hours each day when he engaged with work, he could contribute to a project, solve defined problems, and feel momentarily competent in a world that otherwise left him powerless.

This isn't about using work as escape. It's about recognizing that human beings need both purpose and structure to function—especially during crisis.

The compartmentalization trap

"Just compartmentalize," well-meaning friends will tell you. "Leave your personal problems at home when you get to work."

This is both impossible and unwise.

The idea that you can or should completely separate your personal and professional selves creates an unsustainable psychological burden. When you're going through hell, pretending you're fine doesn't make you stronger—it makes you brittle.

The real skill isn't compartmentalization. It's selective transparency.

A colleague whose long-term relationship ended unexpectedly didn't broadcast the details to her entire department. But she did have a brief, professional conversation with her immediate manager. She didn't want sympathy; she wanted understanding for the occasional moments when she might need flexibility or when her usual attention to detail might temporarily waver.

Her approach was simple: "I'm going through a difficult personal situation. My commitment to our work remains unchanged, but there may be times in the coming weeks when I might need a bit more flexibility. I'll always ensure my responsibilities are covered."

This approach didn't mark her as unprofessional—it demonstrated her maturity. It created space for her to show up authentically without turning the workplace into a therapy session.

The strategic allocation of energy

During personal crisis, energy becomes your scarcest resource. You simply cannot operate at 100% capacity across all domains of your life. Attempting to do so will ensure you fail at everything.

Instead, you must become ruthlessly strategic about where you direct your limited energy.

In your professional life, this means:

1. **Identifying the non-negotiables**: What tasks genuinely require your attention today versus what can wait until next week?
2. **Eliminating the optional**: This isn't the time for volunteering for extra projects or attending every optional lunch-and-learn.
3. **Seeking support**: Can you partner with a trusted colleague on certain tasks? Can you ask for clearer prioritization from your manager?
4. **Managing expectations**: Proactively communicate adjusted timelines rather than missing deadlines or delivering subpar work.
5. **Finding peace at 80%**: Consciously keep some energy in reserve so you are not running full out all the time and you have some left in the tank when you really need it.

I observed a junior analyst who maintained his core responsibilities during a family emergency, but temporarily stepped back from an optional cross-departmental initiative and asked for a one-week extension on a non-urgent report. This wasn't shirking responsibility—it was allocating limited resources to their highest use.

The power of parallel processing

There's a cognitive phenomenon that explains why work can be particularly valuable during personal crisis: parallel processing.

When your conscious mind is occupied with familiar professional tasks, your subconscious continues processing the emotional weight of your personal situation. This is why solutions to personal dilemmas often arrive when you're engaged in unrelated activities.

Many young professionals I've counseled have found that their most productive workdays often yielded the greatest clarity about their personal challenges. The mental space created by focusing on a spreadsheet, presentation, or client call allowed their subconscious to work through emotional knots that seemed impossible when directly confronted. This isn't avoidance. It's allowing different parts of your brain to work on different problems simultaneously.

The distinction between refuge and escape

There's a critical difference between finding refuge in work and using work as escape. One heals; the other harms.

Work becomes destructive escape when you use it to avoid processing necessary emotions or making crucial personal decisions. The analyst who volunteers for every project and stays at the office until midnight following a relationship breakdown isn't finding balance—they're postponing grief that will eventually demand its due.

Work becomes constructive refuge when it provides temporary structure and purpose that helps you gather strength for the personal battles you're facing. It's not about avoiding the pain—it's about creating space where you can momentarily set it aside and remember other aspects of your identity.

The key question: Is your work supporting your overall functioning during crisis, or is it enabling denial?

The growth opportunity in personal crisis

Personal crisis, managed thoughtfully, doesn't just damage your professional development—it can accelerate it in unexpected ways.

I've watched young professionals who navigated significant personal challenges emerge with deeper capacity in several crucial areas:

- Their emotional intelligence sharpened as they became more attuned to the unspoken struggles colleagues might be carrying
- Their prioritization skills improved as they learned to distinguish between genuinely important tasks and merely urgent ones
- Their authenticity increased as they learned the right level of appropriate vulnerability
- Their resilience multiplied through consistent practice under pressure

Crisis reveals what truly matters, and that clarity—painful as it is to acquire—makes you a more focused, empathetic, and effective professional.

The care and feeding of your support system

No one navigates dual crises alone. Your ability to maintain professional effectiveness during personal turmoil depends largely on the strength of your support system.

This system needs to span both domains of your life:

- Professional supports (a trusted manager, mentor, or colleague) who can provide flexibility and understanding
- Personal supports who respect your need to maintain professional engagement

The most dangerous mistake is neglecting either side of this equation. The young professional who tries to manage everything at work without asking for any accommodation will eventually collapse under the weight. The friend or family member who demands your complete attention while dismissing your work responsibilities creates unsustainable tension.

The most effective approach I've observed involves cultivating both: a core relationship at work with someone who understands your temporary limitations, and personal connections who recognize the importance of maintaining professional continuity. Neither should expect perfection, and both should recognize the importance of the other.

The timeline of recovery

Perhaps the most challenging aspect of managing work during personal crisis is navigating the mismatch between external and internal timelines.

From the outside, there's often an expectation that you'll "get back to normal" once the acute phase of crisis passes—after the funeral, after the breakup is a few weeks old, after the medical treatment concludes.

But internal recovery follows a different clock. You may appear functional long before you feel fully restored. The grief, adjustment, or healing continues invisibly long after external markers of crisis have disappeared.

This creates a difficult balancing act. You must gradually resume full professional functioning while still honoring your ongoing internal process. This requires:

- Periodic reassessment of your capacity as circumstances evolve
- Appropriate communication about your changing needs

- Gradual resumption of full workload that prioritizes high-value activities
- Patience with yourself when progress isn't linear

Many professionals I've counseled have found it helpful to have an honest check-in conversation with their manager a few weeks after returning to normal duties—not to ask for continued accommodation, but to ensure alignment on expectations during the recovery phase. This isn't weakness—it's mature self-awareness.

Finding your way forward

There is no perfect formula for balancing professional commitments during personal crisis. What works for one person—or one crisis—may not work for another. But there are principles that can guide your path:

1. **Accept the tension**: There will always be conflict between personal and professional demands during crisis. Accepting this tension rather than expecting it to disappear reduces its power to distress you.
2. **Seek integration, not separation**: Rather than trying to completely compartmentalize, look for appropriate ways to acknowledge your situation and adapt your professional approach accordingly.
3. **Redefine success temporarily**: During crisis, "success" might mean meeting basic deadlines rather than exceeding every expectation. Focus on the "must-do's" versus the "nice-to-haves" you would typically accomplish or deliver. This approach isn't lowering standards—it's adapting them to reality.
4. **Use work purposefully**: Engage with your professional life not as escape but as a domain where you can still experience competence, contribution, and connection during an otherwise chaotic time.
5. **Find meaning in the duality**: The ability to function professionally while navigating personal crisis isn't just a survival skill—it's a profound demonstration of human capacity for resilience.

For many early and mid-career professionals I've observed, work wasn't an inconvenient obligation during personal crisis. It was, unexpectedly, a lifeline—a place where for a few hours each day, they could reconnect with aspects of their identity and purpose beyond the immediate crisis.

This isn't a path anyone would choose. But when it finds you—as it eventually finds us all—know that it's possible to navigate both territories, not perfectly, but well enough to preserve what matters in each.

EXERCISE: THE CRISIS-READY CAREER PLAN

Don't wait for crisis to develop your capacity to navigate personal and professional pressures simultaneously. Prepare now:

1. Create a "critical functions" document outlining which aspects of your role are genuinely essential versus those that could be temporarily paused during personal emergency.
2. Identify 1-2 colleagues who understand your work well enough to help cover urgent matters if necessary.
3. List your current support system in both personal and professional domains. Where are the gaps that would become problematic during crisis?
4. **Identify your early warning signals.** List three behavioral changes that might indicate your personal situation is beginning to affect your professional performance (e.g., missed deadlines, uncharacteristic errors, withdrawal from interaction).
5. Reflect on past challenges where personal issues affected your work. What strategies were most effective? What would you do differently next time?

QUESTION TO REFLECT ON

What aspect of your work provides the greatest sense of meaning, purpose, or stability? How might this element serve as an anchor during personal turbulence rather than an additional burden?

FIRST STEP

Choose one person in your professional life whom you would trust during personal crisis. This might be a mentor, a slightly more senior colleague, or a peer you particularly respect. Schedule a coffee with them in the next month with no agenda other than strengthening the relationship. The time to build support systems is before you need them.

YOU EARNED IT, BE PROUD OF IT

A personal reflection by
John Pierce

I earned a black belt in Taekwondo when I was living in Cincinnati, Ohio. I'd always been interested in martial arts but had never committed to it. Then I found a dojo—a school—and started to go in the evenings. After a couple of years, I realized I had learned a lot about the art and about myself.

My dojo had a lot of really good fighters. And I really enjoyed sparring. That was the fun part of the classes.

By contrast, I didn't like forms, which are a sequence of fighting movements performed to develop skills and prepare you to fight. In fact, I had to retake my black belt test because I didn't put enough effort into my forms. I just liked sparring. Even when I ended up being somewhat of a leader at the school, my focus stayed on sparring.

What I discovered was a lesson that goes beyond this experience. It's this. When you find something that you really like, like sparring, you owe it to yourself to stick with it. Become proficient at it. Enjoy it. At the same time, expect there will be aspects of it that you don't enjoy or even care about. But do what it takes to get to the part that matters to you. I wound up doing the forms because that was part of what I had to do to earn my black belt. That's what it took so I could spar with fighters who made Taekwondo fun and challenging for me.

The second message that I hope comes through is that I earned what I got. In this case, I earned the black belt. Everything you have, you've earned. It's not given to you. It's not your right. It didn't come easily. Don't let anyone under any circumstance diminish what you've earned.

Whether you make the effort to earn subject matter expertise, institutional knowledge, physical prowess, a language, or anything else that is in your quiver, the issue is that you did it. Whatever you accomplish, you've accomplished it because you've earned it. Nothing was given to you. No one has the right to mock it, diminish it, or make less of it.

Too often, society tries to minimize our accomplishments or someone in your circle makes light of what you've done. Let's not let that happen. Be proud of what you've earned.

20

BECOMING THE LIGHT: HOW YOUR TRANSFORMATION ILLUMINATES OTHERS

What's the point of all this work? The fear you face down. The pressure you transform into power. The odds you overcome. The darkness you navigate and the light you surround yourself in.

Is it just for a bigger title? A fatter paycheck? A more impressive LinkedIn profile? If that's all you gain, I've failed you as a mentor—and you've cheated yourself of the most profound reward of the journey.

The ultimate measure of your transformation isn't what you've achieved for yourself. It's who you've become and how that illuminates the path for others. That includes not just people in the workplace. It includes the people at home, your friends, acquaintances, and even strangers who witness parts of your journey.

Think about the mentors who changed your life. The ones who saw something in you that you couldn't yet see yourself. The ones who told you the hard truths when everyone else was feeding you comfortable lies. The ones who believed in you not despite your struggles but because of how you faced them.

Did they help you because it advanced their careers? Because it boosted their egos? Because some corporate policy mandated that they check a "mentoring" box on their performance review?

No. They helped you because transformation isn't meant to end with the individual. It's meant to ripple outward, touching lives you may never even meet. Like you and me.

The Transformation Cycle: From Mentored to Mentor

Consider a moment when a mentor's insight transforms not just your situation, but your understanding of why overcoming challenges matters in the first place.

A senior financial professional I know shared his transformative experience with a mentor early in his career. As a junior analyst preparing for his first major client presentation, he found himself paralyzed with fear—convinced he'd fail spectacularly and be exposed as an impostor.

His mentor noticed his uncharacteristic silence during the prep meeting and asked him to stay behind when everyone else filed out. Instead of offering empty reassurances, this mentor shared his own nearly identical experience from fifteen years earlier, complete with the physical symptoms, the self-doubt, and the certainty that his career would implode.

"I'm not telling you this to make you feel better," the mentor explained. "I'm telling you because one day, you'll be the experienced one, and some talented young professional will be standing where you are now, thinking they're the only one who's ever felt this way. When that moment comes, remember today."

That conversation didn't just help the young advisor through a difficult presentation. It fundamentally shifted his understanding of the purpose behind overcoming challenges. Years later, when he found himself mentoring a promising team member through a similar crisis of confidence, he realized: We don't just overcome our challenges for ourselves. We overcome them so we can reach back and guide others through their own dark passages.

This is the transformation cycle that gives meaning to our professional journeys. From mentored to mentor. From guided to guide. From receiving light to becoming it.

The Three Phases of Illumination

Becoming a source of light for others isn't something that happens accidentally or all at once. It unfolds through three distinct phases, each requiring specific commitments:

Phase 1: Bearing Witness

The first phase begins with simply acknowledging others' struggles without trying to minimize, fix, or erase them. This sounds easier than it is. When we see someone in professional pain—whether from rejection, failure, or uncertainty—our instinct is often to quickly reassure them or steer them toward "positive thinking."

True illumination starts not with dispensing solutions but with bearing witness to reality. "Yes, this is difficult. Yes, this hurts. No, I won't look away from your struggle."

Remember Sarah from our earlier discussion about pressure? The one facing an impossible deadline? What she needed first wasn't a time management system. She needed someone to acknowledge the legitimacy of her overwhelm without immediately jumping to solutions.

The ability to bear witness comes directly from your own journey. Having faced your own fears, you can sit with others in theirs without being overcome. Having navigated your own dark passages, you can validate someone else's experience without needing to minimize it.

This is harder than it sounds. We're conditioned to offer immediate solutions, to say "it's not that bad," to rush people through discomfort. Resisting this impulse—creating space for someone to fully experience their challenge—is a profound act of professional compassion.

Phase 2: Revealing the Map

Once you've genuinely acknowledged someone's reality, you earn the right to share what you've learned from your own journey. Not as a lecture or a "here's what you should do," but as a map offered by someone who has walked a similar path.

"Here's what the terrain ahead might look like. These are the obstacles I encountered. These are the resources that helped me. These are the places I stumbled."

Note that revealing the map isn't the same as dictating someone's route. You're not telling them exactly where to step or how fast to move. You're giving them orientation so they can make their own choices with clearer vision.

The map you share comes directly from your own transformation. Your setbacks and recoveries, your failures and breakthroughs—these aren't just personal war stories. They're trail markers for those who follow.

I witnessed this distinction powerfully when observing two senior executives mentoring junior talent. The first spent meetings dispensing wisdom from on high, telling junior staff exactly what to do in each situation. The second shared his own career inflection points—the mistakes he'd made, the lessons he'd learned, the questions he wished he'd asked sooner.

Months later, the difference was clear: Those mentored by the first executive came back repeatedly for specific instructions. Those mentored by the second had developed their own navigation systems, calling on their mentor not for directions but for perspective on the maps they were creating themselves.

Phase 3: Walking Alongside

The final phase of becoming light for others isn't about standing in front pointing the way. It's about walking alongside, illuminating the path through your presence and example.

This is where your transformation becomes most powerful—when you demonstrate rather than dictate. When your actions embody the principles you've learned and the values that are dear to you. When you show rather than tell.

Walking alongside means being honest about your ongoing challenges. It means acknowledging that you don't have all the answers but you're committed to the same journey of growth. It means sharing not just your successes but your continued struggles in real-time.

I've watched professionals sabotage their influence by creating false images of perfection. They position themselves as having "arrived"—beyond the challenges that others face. This doesn't inspire; it distances. No one feels connected to someone claiming to have transcended all struggles.

Far more powerful is the leader who acknowledges their continued growth while demonstrating consistent principles. "I'm still learning too, but here's what I know for certain... Here's what I'm practicing daily... Here's where I'm still stretching myself..."

This kind of authentic illumination creates what anthropologists call "legitimate peripheral participation"—the ability for newcomers to engage in genuine practice alongside more experienced practitioners. It's how true mastery is transmitted in any domain, from ancient craft guilds to modern professional communities.

The Reluctant Light

Here's what stops most people from becoming light for others: they're waiting until they feel "finished" with their own transformation. Until they've conquered all their fears, mastered all their pressures, overcome all their odds. Until they've "arrived" at some imagined destination of perfect confidence.

This is like waiting until you've crossed the entire ocean before helping someone else who's drowning ten feet away. Your incomplete journey is still infinitely valuable to someone who hasn't begun theirs.

I've worked with countless mid-career professionals who dismiss their potential to guide others with statements like:

"I'm still figuring things out myself." "Who am I to advise anyone else?" "I haven't achieved enough to be a mentor."

These statements reveal a fundamental misunderstanding of how human development works. None of us ever fully "arrives." There is no perfect, polished final state where all growth is complete. The most valuable guides aren't those who have finished their journey but those who are actively engaged in theirs—with enough experience to offer perspective but enough humility to remember how difficult the path can be.

Your transformation doesn't need to be complete to illuminate others. It simply needs to be authentic, ongoing, and visible.

Reciprocal Illumination

Here's something they don't tell you about becoming light for others: it illuminates your own path with equal power.

There's a phenomenon cognitive scientists call the "protégé effect." When you teach something to others, you deepen your own understanding. When you articulate lessons from your experience, you clarify them for yourself. When you guide someone through their challenges, you develop new insights into your own.

This isn't just a nice bonus; it's the completion of the transformation cycle. The light you share doesn't diminish yours—it magnifies it. Each person you help clarifies your own vision. Each struggle you witness heightens your self-awareness. Each map you share refines your own navigation.

I've experienced this phenomenon repeatedly throughout my career. Moments when I thought I fully understood a principle—like transforming pressure into power or finding confidence in the shadows—only to discover new dimensions while helping someone else apply it to their unique circumstances. This reciprocal illumination isn't accidental; it's how human development is designed to work. We learn through teaching. We receive through giving. We clarify through explaining. We discover through guiding.

From Success to Significance

Early in your career, success might have seemed like enough—the promotions, the recognition, the financial rewards. But as your journey progresses, something shifts. The question changes from "How far can I go?" to "How much can I contribute?"

This shift isn't about abandoning ambition. It's about elevating it from success to significance.

Success is measured by what you achieve. Significance is measured by what you enable others to achieve. Success leaves footprints. Significance leaves a path that others can follow. Significance is your legacy.

The ultimate expression of your transformation isn't a perfect performance of confidence, power, or resilience. It's becoming a source of light that enables others to find their way forward—sometimes following your path, sometimes creating entirely new ones that you couldn't have imagined.

The Questions That Matter

As we near the end of this journey together, I want to leave you with the questions that matter most—the ones that will reveal how thoroughly your transformation has taken hold:

- Who sees possibility in themselves because of how you see them?
- Whose darkness feels less absolute because you've shared light from your journey?
- Who makes better decisions because you've revealed your map?
- Whose courage grows in the presence of yours?
- What potential in others gets unlocked because you believe in it?

These questions aren't meant to burden you with responsibility for others' journeys. That's not how illumination works. You don't drag people forward; you light the way so they can move themselves.

But these questions do reframe how you measure the worth of your professional life. Not by titles achieved or wealth accumulated, but by darkness dispelled and potential unleashed.

Not everyone will choose to become light for others. Many will hoard their hard-won wisdom, viewing it as competitive advantage rather than shared resource. They'll climb to heights of individual success while casting no illumination for those who follow.

That's their choice. What's yours?

Will your transformation end with you, or will it ripple outward? Will you keep your maps hidden, or will you share them with fellow travelers? Will you measure your worth only by your achievements, or also by the achievements you enable in others?

The answers to these questions don't just determine the impact of your career. They define its meaning.

EXERCISE: THE ILLUMINATION INVENTORY

1. Identify three specific challenges you've overcome in your professional journey that might provide valuable perspective to others.
2. For each challenge, articulate the key insights that helped you navigate it successfully.
3. List three people in your professional orbit who might benefit from your perspective on these challenges.
4. Create a specific, actionable plan for sharing your relevant experience with each person in a way that respects their agency and honors their unique journey.

QUESTION TO REFLECT ON

What wisdom have you gained through struggle that you've been hesitant to share with others? What holds you back from becoming a more deliberate source of illumination for those around you?

FIRST STEP

Identify someone in your professional life who appears to be facing a challenge similar to one you've navigated. Schedule a coffee conversation focused not on giving advice, but on bearing witness to their experience and offering your map only if they express interest in seeing it.

"YOU LOOK LIKE YOU'RE FROM OHIO."

A personal reflection by

John Pierce

"**W**ell, Mike, I am from Ohio."

That was my response to my first mentor, at least the first one who wasn't one of my parents. I had arrived, literally and metaphorically. I was now in the big Philadelphia office at Merrill Lynch, after being in the outskirts for five years.

On that first day in Philadelphia, Mike walked me down to Joseph A. Banks, the clothing retailer. Then, he bought me a bunch of suits, so I didn't look like I was from Ohio.

Mike's generosity went beyond the suits. He became my mentor and helped me think, act, and look like I belonged in a big East Coast financial center. As a kid raised in Ohio, educated in Ohio through undergraduate, and having lived my life with all my friends and family there: how was I to know what this part of my journey required? That's where Mike changed how I saw myself and my future.

With 30 years under his belt, Mike had an incredible amount of wisdom, insights, and practical advice to give me as I took on and mastered the responsibilities and nuances of my role. That first day is marked forever in my memory because it vividly illustrates the outsized impact a mentor can have on you. A mentor is volunteering to show up for you. They're focusing on you, not on themselves. That is an incredible gift.

Mike, thanks. Your care and feeding of me has helped scores of others with each ripple and new promotion or advancement.

Keep in mind, mentors aren't coaches or sounding boards. They provide tough love. They can guide you to making changes based on their experience—and it's for your benefit, not theirs. Don't take umbrage when your mentor is advising you to take actions that are outside your comfort zone. That's the point of the relationship. This isn't cheerleading. It's the stretch strategies that account for why great mentors lead to great careers. Appreciate your mentor and embrace the challenges.

How do you pay a mentor? Your progress is their compensation. Your progress is their reward. That's why it's important that you execute where appropriate on your mentor's recommendations. Communicate with them as you face challenges or roadblocks so you can get results. The tacit understanding is that if you don't make progress, a mentor may drop you.

Disclaimer: Use good judgement when you choose or accept a mentor because if you have a bad mentor, they can do immeasurable damage to you and your career. Bad mentors have you do things for their benefit, not yours. If you ever get an inkling that you have a mentor working with their self-interest in mind and not yours, it's time to cut that relationship quickly, albeit gracefully.

ASSESSMENT

PIERCE CHECK AND RESET MINDSET TEST: A SELF-TALK TRANSFORMATION EXERCISE

The way we talk to ourselves shapes everything we do. Our internal dialogue—the constant conversation we have with ourselves—acts as a filter through which we see opportunities, face challenges, and interact with the world around us. While we all experience similar circumstances in life, it's our self-talk that determines whether we see obstacles or opportunities, whether we shrink from challenges or rise to meet them.

This exercise will help you discover and reshape your internal dialogue, firmly setting the foundation for unshakable confidence in your personal and professional life.

Purpose

This assessment will help you:

- Identify your current patterns of self-talk
- Create powerful, personalized affirmations that resonate with your authentic voice
- Develop a practical tool for maintaining confidence in challenging situations

Tip: The words in all capital letters are your key to crafting self-talk that can program your mind for success.

Step 1: Word Selection

Review each of the seven columns below in the Word Bank. These words represent different aspects of personal power and resilience. For each column, select one or two words that naturally align with your speaking style—words you could comfortably use in your daily thoughts.

1 UNSHAKABLE	2 CONFIDENCE	3 AGAINST THE ODDS
Steadfast	Self-assurance	Overcome adversity
Resolute	Certainty	Beat the odds
Unyielding	Poise	Defy expectations
Firm	Self-belief	Swim upstream
Immovable	Conviction	Fight an uphill battle
Unflinching	Composure	Push through obstacles
Inflexible	Assurance	Persevere through hardship
Indomitable	Courage	Rise above challenges
Unwavering	Trust	Prevail despite setbacks
Ironclad	Faith	Endure all slings
Unrelenting	Power	Break through barriers
Rock-solid	Self-reliance	Face down unfavorable circumstances
Tenacious	Optimism	Triumph over challenges
Enduring	Determination	Surmount the insurmountable
Steely	Self-esteem	Struggle through disadvantages

4 FEAR	5 PRESSURE	6 THRIVE	7 SUCCESS
Overwhelm	Stress	Flourish	Achievement
Anxiety	Strain	Prosper	Victory
Concern	Tension	Succeed	Accomplishment
Dread	Burden	Excel	Triumph
Apprehension	Demand	Advance	Prosperity
Panic	Overload	Grow	Fulfillment
Trepidation	Duress	Progress	Attainment
Doubt	Weight	Soar	Fruition
Alarm	Anxiety	Blossom	Advancement
Phobia	Constraint	Expand	Progress
Unease	Compulsion	Develop	Realization
Paranoia	Challenge	Surge	Win
Disquiet	Urgency	Achieve	Mastery
Intimidation	Implosion	Radiate	Excel
Foreboding	Intensity	Win	Breakthrough

Step 2: Create Your Power Statement

Combine your chosen words to create a personal "I am" statement. This statement should feel natural when you say it and inspire confidence when you hear it.

The formula is:

I am **COLUMN 1** in my **COLUMN 2** to

COLUMN 3, 4, AND 5

so I **COLUMN 6** and **COLUMN 7** .

By the way, this formula is so customizable that you could create 170,859,375 possible unique combinations of words for "I am" statements following this format! This ensures that you can find combinations that truly resonate with your personal style and situation, while still maintaining the powerful structure of this affirmative self-talk.

Examples

I am **UNYIELDING** in my **FAITH** to

RISE ABOVE CHALLENGES, DOUBT, AND TENSION

so I **EXCEL** and **WIN** .

I am **INDOMITABLE** in my **DETERMINATION** to

OVERCOME ADVERSITY, APPREHENSION, AND ANXIETY

so I **PROSPER** and enjoy the **FRUITION** of my dreams.

I am **STEADFAST** in my **SELF-ASSURANCE** to

SWIM UPSTREAM, PUSHING PAST OVERWHELM AND STRESS

until I **FLOURISH** and achieve **VICTORY** !

I am **ROCK-SOLID** in my **CONVICTION** to

DEFY EXPECTATIONS, TRANSFORMING TREPIDATION AND URGENCY INTO FUEL

that helps me **SOAR** toward **MASTERY** .

I am **TENACIOUS** in my **COURAGE** to

BREAK THROUGH BARRIERS, CONVERTING PANIC AND STRAIN INTO STRENGTH

as I **PROGRESS** toward **FULFILLMENT** .

I am **UNWAVERING** in my **SELF-BELIEF** to

PERSEVERE THROUGH HARDSHIP, MOVING BEYOND DREAD AND BURDEN

until I **BLOSSOM** into **PROSPERITY** .

I am **RESOLUTE** in my **OPTIMISM** to

TRIUMPH OVER CHALLENGES, TRANSFORMING DISQUIET AND INTENSITY

into power that **DRIVES** my **BREAKTHROUGH** .

I am **STEELY** in my **TRUST** to

SURMOUNT THE INSURMOUNTABLE, CHANNELING UNEASE AND DEMANDS

into energy that **POWERS** my **ADVANCEMENT** .

Step 3: Implementation

1. Save your power statements somewhere easily accessible—your phone's notes app, a small notebook, or even as a background image on your device.
2. Set specific times to practice your statements:
   - First thing in the morning to set your intention for the day
   - Before important meetings or challenging situations
   - At the end of the day to reinforce your mindset
3. Experiment with different word combinations to create statements that match various situations in your life.

Making It Work for You

Remember, the most powerful self-talk is the kind that feels authentic to you. Choose combinations that energize and inspire you while still feeling true to your voice. Your self-talk will evolve as you do, becoming an increasingly powerful tool for personal and professional growth. These affirmations will serve as a foundation for implementing the new approaches you have learned have unshakable confidence by facing fear, transforming pressure into power, and thriving against all odds!

ASSESSMENT

PIERCE RESOURCE INDEX AND TACTICAL PLAN

Twelve areas of your life contribute to the resources available to you when pressure is mounting, and you must dig deep into what you've been banking. It's certainly not all financial, in fact, there are many other areas, as you'll see below, that contribute to your ability to meet and master the challenges you face.

This index is an opportunity for you to frankly assess yourself and then build two lists: Resource Strengths and Resource Building. Once you have those identified, you'll be guided to use what you have and add to your stockpile. With an action plan, you'll be stronger every day in almost every way. And, you will be able to count on yourself to be resilient and bounce forward when you're going through challenging times.

Here's how to use this index.

On a scale of five to one, rate yourself in response to each question in Step One. Depending on the question, the 5-point scale, may mean

5: Abundant, Very Strong, Very Frequently

4: Ample, Strong, Frequently

3: Sufficient, Satisfactory, Sometimes

2: Limited, Weak, Infrequently

1: Scarce, Very Weak, Very Infrequently

Step 1: Assessing Your Resources

For each resource below, you will find three questions to help you assess what you have that helps you face pressure, stress, and the need to provide support for the choices you would like to make.

Cognitive Resources

___ How confident are you in your ability to solve complex problems at work?

___ How well do you understand and retain new information in your role?

___ How quickly can you adapt to changing work environments or requirements?

Emotional Resources

___ How well do you manage your emotions during stressful situations?

___ How often are you genuinely enthusiastic about work and your career?

___ How easily do you recover from emotional challenges in the workplace?

Physical Well-being

___ How often do you feel physically energized to complete your work tasks?

___ How satisfied are you with your physical health and its impact on your job performance?

___ How much effort do you make to increase your physical well-being?

Spiritual Resources

___ How connected do you feel to a greater sense of purpose in your work?

___ How much does your work align with your core values or beliefs?

___ How much inner peace or calm can you access during challenging times at work?

Mindset

___ How positive is your outlook on mastering challenges that arise from work?

___ How open are you to learning from your mistakes or failures at work?

___ How confident are you in your ability to succeed?

Habits

___ How consistent are you in following daily routines that contribute to work success?

___ How well do your current work habits support your productivity and focus?

___ How intentional are you in maintaining healthy work-life balance habits?

Family

___ How supportive is your family regarding your career goals and work responsibilities?

___ How much time are you able to dedicate to family without sacrificing work commitments?

___ How much do you feel your family contributes to your overall well-being at work?

Friends

___ How much support do your friends provide when you're facing work challenges?

___ How often do you feel your friends' encouragement and regard for your career?

___ How much do your friends contribute to your emotional resilience at work?

Social Resources

___ How strong are your interpersonal relationships?

___ How well do you feel integrated into organizations or associations related to work?

___ How often do you engage in social activities that relieve work-related stress?

Community

___ How involved are you in your community outside of work?

___ How much does your community involvement positively impact your sense of balance in life?

___ How well do you feel your community connections contribute to your professional growth?

Business or Alumni Network

___ How frequently do you rely on your business or alumni network for professional support?

___ How strong are your professional relationships within your business or alumni network?

___ How much has your network contributed to your career advancement, leads for your company, or opportunities for partnerships?

Financial Resources

___ How secure do you feel in your financial situation related to supporting your career goals?

___ How well are you able to manage your finances to reduce work-related stress?

___ How confident are you in your financial planning for your professional future?

Step 2: Finding the Resource Gaps

Now, you get to interpret the results of your assessment. At this step, you are going to review your scores across the different resource categories and look for gaps, so that you'll be able to create a tailored action plan that fills those gaps and strengthens your existing resources.

RESOURCES STRENGTHS LIST

First, identify your strengths. Jot down the areas where you scored a four or five. When you have time, come up with the specific details that support those ratings. Your Resources Strengths List can be the first place you look when you are feeling pressure and need to reassure yourself that you are well-resourced in at least some areas that help you manage it.

RESOURCE BUILDING LIST

Second, identify your weak areas. Jot down the areas where you scored a one, two, or three. When you have time, come up with the specific details and actions that will help you build more resources in those areas—or identify where you can compensate for what's missing (perhaps in the family or physical well-being sections) that simply cannot be filled in. Keep in mind that no one has a perfect score and never will. That's why we have so many ways to provide ourselves with the resources we need.

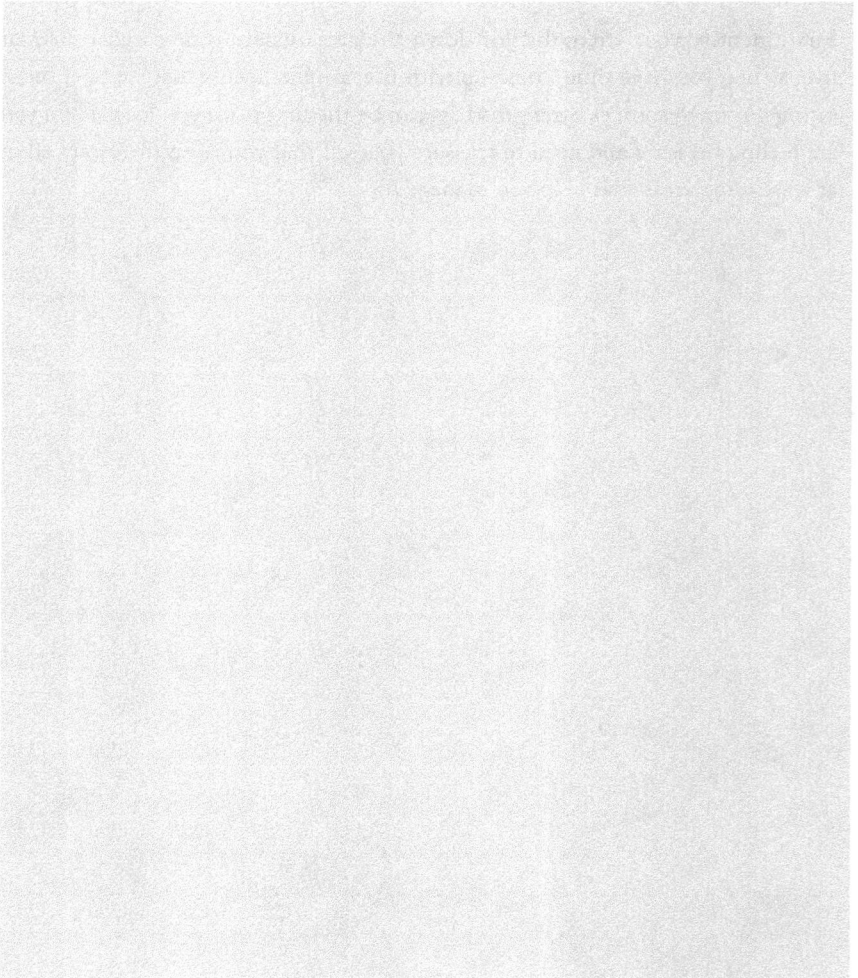

Step 3: Connect the Dots

If you're completing this index in a live training, your leader will facilitate a discussion about how gaps in one category (e.g., financial or social resources) might affect your overall well-being or performance. Sometimes, deficits in one area can spill over and create stress in others.

If you're using this material on your own, you may find some inspiration and problem-solving tips by going to a trusted source such as TED Talks (https:// www.ted.com/talks). Use the resource headings in this assessment or each question (family, friends, financial, physical well-being, and the others) to identify the keywords that will help you search the TED platform for great content.

Step 4: Set Goals for Resource Development

Let's prioritize your resource building. Choose one or two resource categories to focus on first, based on the greatest need or the areas most relevant to your current work situation. For example, if you need to increase your network so you can bring in new leads or develop new referral sources, then you may want to focus on building your business and alumni connections. Or, if you can't get out of bed in the morning, consider working on your physical well-being.

Priority Resource Category #1: _____

Priority Resource Category #2: _____

What you choose as your priorities and how you choose to fill the gaps are personal choices that not only move you forward but also show you how resourceful you can be! Don't let anyone choose for you when you can choose for yourself. For example, to increase your alumni connections, you can join your school's alumni association and become active in some committee that get you involved in a way that's nourishing and fruitful. On the other hand, you can use LinkedIn to reach out to alumni and arrange some online coffee chats to learn more about the people who may be geographically distant but intellectually or workwise more aligned with your interests.

Pick your two to three priorities and decide what outcomes or goals will make you feel better resourced in those areas.

Then, set SMART Goals. Create Specific, Measurable, Achievable, Relevant, and Time-bound goals to improve in your prioritized areas. For example, if you scored low in "networking," a SMART goal might be: "Attend one professional event each month and connect with three new people." Create milestones so you are clear that you are making progress every week. Milestones are simply your forecasted result from a group of smaller, achievable steps. Thus, your plan doesn't add pressure to your life, and it's fun to see how you achieve your goals over time.

SMART Goal #1: _____

   ❑ Milestone #1: _____

   ❑ Milestone #2: _____

   ❑ Milestone #3: _____

   ❑ Milestone #4: _____

SMART Goal #2: _____

   ❑ Milestone #1: _____

   ❑ Milestone #2: _____

   ❑ Milestone #3: _____

   ❑ Milestone #4: _____

SMART Goal #3: _____

   ❑ Milestone #1: _____

   ❑ Milestone #2: _____

   ❑ Milestone #3: _____

   ❑ Milestone #4: _____

Step 5: Create an Internal and External Support System

Use your resources. Most resources get stronger when you use them. For example, when you increase your awareness of good habits, you may find that you feel more resilient, which lets you learn new things with less anxiety. The logic is simple. When you take care of the little things, you can be fully present for the big challenges you face. If you enjoy your social or community time, you can use that energy to tackle obstacles at work.

Jot down your thoughts about how can you use your internal strengths to support the areas where you are weaker.

You may also consider mentorship or guidance to build skills in each area. Consider approaching managers, coaches, or colleagues who clearly excel in areas where you have gaps. Some areas necessarily call for external support. For example, networking or joining a non-profit service group can help fill in social or community gaps.

Jot down your thoughts about how you can approach people you know, people who might be open to connecting with you on LinkedIn, or organizations that are interesting to you.

Create SMART goals with milestones so you can manage your progress and celebrate your results.

Step 6: Develop a Mindset of Growth and Patience

Your SMART goals and milestones are the tactical action plan you need to succeed. However, you also need some other essential components. Plan to build these so you can stay in the game long enough to enjoy the results of your plan.

1. Build faith in the process: How will you cultivate the necessary patience and trust that progress will come over time? Will approaches like mindfulness or meditation help you stay on course when things feel uncertain or slow-moving?

2. Promote a growth mindset: How will you encourage yourself to develop or keep a mindset that focuses on growth and learning rather than fixed abilities? If you have an "all or nothing" way of thinking, you'll need to restructure that so you can appreciate incremental progress. How will you plan for setbacks or slower progress in filling gaps? Spend time now planning for the hiccups that are part of the journey, so a lapse in progress does not become a collapse of your resource building efforts.

Step 7: Schedule Regular Check-ins

Appreciation and problem-solving ideally are a part of your productivity habits. On a weekly basis, plan to assess your progress and adjust your action plan if necessary. Celebrate your wins! Recognizing and celebrating all improvements or small victories along the way will boost morale and reinforce positive behavior. You might do this by yourself, with a buddy, or with your mentor.

Last tip: Be resourceful as you build your resources. Use every experience and encounter to build your unshakable confidence!

HOW TO LOVE AND HATE INSTITUTIONS— AND OTHER WAYS TO SURPRISE YOURSELF

Let me tell you something they don't teach in business school: success isn't just about goals, systems, tactics, and metrics. Even though you've heard or read the same advice a million times. Set out a plan. Follow the plan. Take action every day to implement the plan. When you arrive at your goal, make a new plan. Rinse. Repeat.

That advice is not just wrong. It's dangerously incomplete.

Anyone who says "always follow the plan" or "work is life" is delivering an unseasoned assessment of what you can do to make money and really enjoy the journey. They're missing half the picture. The unspoken truth? At least half of your success is going to arise from unexpected sources or unplanned circumstances. The chance meetings. The serendipitous connections. The accidents that teach you more than intentions or a plan ever could.

The most successful people I've met don't just have rigid systems—they have finely-tuned antennas for capturing the unexpected. They know when to stick to the plan and when to throw it out entirely. Let me show you how to develop this capacity for productive surprise.

Leverage your HUH moments

Get ready to take action when you have a "*HUH?!?!*" moment. You know, when you're living your life, and see something that provokes you to think: "what the heck is that?" Those are very, very promising moments.

I remember walking through a local street fair one weekend in the DC area, where each of my three kids attended and graduated from George Washington University. Under one of the vendor tents, I bought a belt from Jon Wye and his wife. I am a HUGE supporter of small business. In fact, I believe we all need to commit to buy local.

After that first purchase from the Wyes and over past 15+ years, I've purchased lots of great stuff from them but that's not the reason for including them in this story. Here's the reason. Back in the day, when I bought that belt, Jon used this "slidey thing" when I handed over my credit card. I thought, "HUH—what the heck is that?"

It was the first time I saw a "Square." I thought, wow, how cool. But here's the lesson: I liked the device and thought it was cool…. so I bought some stock in XYZ. Score!

That "HUH" moment—that flash of curiosity about something that doesn't quite fit your existing mental models—is often the universe handing you an opportunity disguised as confusion.

Most people brush these moments aside. They're too busy following their plans to notice the unexpected. But the most successful people I know treat these moments like gold. They pause. They investigate. They ask questions. And sometimes, they act.

Break stuff (or at least watch those who do)

I'm always captivated by first movers that just break the mold.

I invested early in TSLA simply because in Elon Musk I saw a brilliant entrepreneur who lacks a normal person's fear of failure, much like Steve Jobs did. The guy is willing to break stuff, think differently, and be called a freak.

He thought traditional car dealerships were stupid because the cost of inventory was too much overhead. But, he was completely conventional when it came to taking government subsidies to get his ventures off the ground, government rebates to get his cars on the road, and government contracts to pay for rocket ships. He has a "break *and* partake" mentality. Pretty smart!

The most influential companies and leaders share this quality—a willingness to break existing paradigms while being strategic about which established systems to leverage.

Look around your industry. Who's breaking things? Who's asking questions nobody else is asking? These aren't just interesting characters—they're living laboratories for what might be possible in your own career.

Learn to lose so you can win

When you invest, holding is the highest value strategy but it can hurt.

As you can tell, I tend to be a value buyer. I hold my equities for a very long time. I don't panic with market swings. I invest in firms that provide game changing products, services, or concepts that I initially find benefit myself and others around me.

I've been long for over 15-years in these names: AAPL, MSFT, GOOG, TSLA, AMZN. They go up, they go down. If they deliver a differentiated offering, I won't be selling.

Some of my investments were world beaters that didn't work out and got passed over. That includes INTC—which I sold on a bunch of calls to lock in a return. NVDA replaced INTC in the Dow 30, which no one in their right mind would have guessed 15 years ago. So, when I say I hold, I didn't say I keep my eyes shut. Freshen up your investment strategy and your acumen. Don't depend on hot tips. Remember, most stocks under $5 are likely to drop to $0. Do your own homework and make decisions that are right for you.

This principle extends far beyond investing. The willingness to accept small, strategic losses while keeping your eye on the bigger picture is what separates those who build lasting success from those who flame out chasing short-term wins.

I do take flyers on stuff that I am willing to lose on. Remember the little red lawn mower that you could not break—Briggs & Stratton? I invested and was up... then lost it all.

Years ago, I read an article in Barrons or Forbes on Russian oil property Gazprom. I bought that and was up big until oil sanctions hit and now it sits in my IRA at $0. Who knows where it goes from there.

A flyer that worked out (so far) is NVDA. I bought it a while back for two main reasons—my son John had a baller computer for gaming and NVDA chips were the magic that made it work. Then, when I started to listen to different podcasts about AI—exciting and scary—it made sense to buy the equity. NVDA worked out. Not everything does.

The best leaders I know aren't afraid to be wrong. They make calculated bets, accept that some will fail, and keep moving forward with new information. They know that the pathway to being spectacularly right sometimes runs through being occasionally wrong.

Banking does not suck

Big banks are not the enemy.

I like to root for underdogs—even when it's easier to mock them or overlook them. Sometimes, first impressions are wrong—and you might think of banks as slow, fragile, or otherwise defective in their practices. Despite what you may understand about the banking sector, they play a unique and necessary role. Liquidity, capital raising, lending, and providing advice for a secure future is critical.

While Bank of America, JP Morgan, UBS, and Wells Fargo went through a lot of growing—and staying—pains at various times, all bounced back and have done a lot of good for individual investors and small business owners.

Here's the deeper lesson: institutions aren't inherently good or bad—they're complex systems with both flaws and strengths. The ability to see both—to simultaneously love and hate the institutions that shape our world—is a surprisingly rare skill.

Most people get stuck in simplistic thinking. Banks are evil. Corporations are greedy. Government is inefficient. These mental shortcuts might feel satisfying, but they blind you to opportunities that live in the nuance.

Love my enemy (and perhaps yours!)

Before I pivot away from financial services let me focus on a firm I loved to hate. LPL is the largest independent financial services firm in the country. I had to compete against LPL's Rich Steinmeier when I led recruiting at Ameriprise, Stifel, and Cetera. The competition got so personal I could swear Steinmeier was trying to get me fired because LPL was relentless about winning.

Sometimes being beaten by the best is a lesson about greatness.

LPL is the largest indy on the street, yet they are also the nimblest. That's because they are organized in a modular manner, so they can pivot and change quickly and efficiently. That's a lot different than turning around a big, old warship.

They could quickly do what it took—get out a new offer, lower a GAF (global administration fee), change payout, whatever it took to get the deal done. All while competitors took days or weeks to act, because those companies were making decisions by committee.

I was very pleased to communicate with Rich when he became the CEO of LPL, ready to crush the next competitor. This capacity—to learn from those who defeat you rather than dismissing them—is remarkably rare. Most people protect their egos by diminishing worthy opponents. "They only won because they cheated." "They got lucky." "They had advantages we didn't."

The most successful people I know do the opposite. They study their losses with genuine curiosity. They extract lessons from competitors that can be applied to their own approach. They're willing to be surprised by what works, even when it contradicts their existing beliefs.

There's nothing small about small business

I mentioned my fondness for small business and that naturally extends to the entrepreneurs who basically create the world we inhabit. When you are looking for personal relationships where people will go the extra mile for you, be grateful for your business, work to earn it every day, and may be even be fun to hang with—think about hiring a small firm rather than whomever comes up first on a Google search because they could pay the most for the top sponsored spot.

Consider the heart, sweat, and brains it took for a small business to survive COVID. Those business owners fought to stay alive. Most did that by becoming more competitive, leaner, and providing transformational value. I came upon a company called Terra (Terrahq.com) that exemplifies doing all that. The owners Remy Bernstein and Cooper Pickett fit that mold. With pure grit and real talent, they built a global resource for digital content, web, and the full range of marketing communications.

What's the lesson here? The most resilient organizations aren't necessarily the largest or most established. They're the ones that combine adaptability with deep commitment to their mission. The ones willing to transform when circumstances demand it, without abandoning their core values.

Connect with good people

Get a guide: a coach, mentor, sherpa, or sounding board.

Since 1999, Fran Johnston has been there for me with coaching, mentoring, and sound boarding. My connection with her has been pivotal because first, she is a quality human being, and of course, she has an earned reputation as a successful change agent and entrepreneur in the coaching world. Fran and her team move leaders that move the world. If you don't see the value of a coach by now, it's on me for not getting it across.

Give thanks

As you are getting to where you want to go, give thanks to those who help you or help you find the resources that you need. I've experienced in life that the best relationships, connections, interactions are referral based. I met Nance Rosen through Chantalle Couba—out of the blue, totally unconnected, as I started to scratch this book out. Without Nance there would be no book. So, while you don't have to write a book to thank others, just be human and thank others that help you.

Amplify

Get beyond the companies you work for, get better connected, and amplify your message via social media platforms. I've been a power user of LinkedIn for years. I'm perturbed that I'm capped at 30,000 followers. I believed in Twitter, pre–X, and have 40k or so followers there.

You might like Instagram or TikTok or another platform—but don't just like it. Meet people on it. Pick your content area. Find the influencers that mirror or oppose your point of view. Comment, praise, argue a bit—don't just like and leave. You might even scroll through their followers and follow the active ones—who will follow you back and build your visibility.

Hone some key messages, put your thoughts in terms that serve your readers, and be consistent. It works if you work it.

The most successful people I know aren't just skilled at what they do—they're intentional about who they connect with. They recognize that no achievement is truly solo, and they build networks of support, challenge, and opportunity.

Hard knocks should be an Ivy League school

You'll never regret a day of education—no matter where it came from. Everything you do and everyone you meet can make you smarter, stronger, faster, and a better version of who you are. Of course, it could also make you bitter, angry, mean, and unforgiving. Your choice. Choose wisely.

No matter how much wisdom you collect from the hard knocks or triumphs in your life, my advice is to use formal education and training programs to give you the thinking skills, work skills, and career building mindset you need to stay fresh along your journey. Most professors or instructors are also consultants, corporate managers, or have connections to industry that they can use to help you get an introduction into a company that otherwise you might not have access to.

As a lifelong learner, I gained significant work skills by earning my masters at the University of London and my doctorate in education from the University of Pennsylvania. I made connections among classmates who were all working professionals. When I reflect on education, I enjoyed being in a "four wall vacuum"—tossing around ideas that will never get put into action in the real world. You might like the pride of pursuing another degree because you want it—which feels very different than attending school because you're required to.

Take advantage of going to a real class, workshop, seminar, or program to learn something new and meet new people when you can. You never know what good things can happen unless you do something or go somewhere that at least a little scary, right?

This is perhaps the most surprising secret of successful people I've observed: they treat every experience—especially difficult ones—as education rather than just endurance. They're constantly extracting lessons, patterns, and insights, even from situations most would simply try to survive.

The true masters transform their hardest knocks into their most valuable credentials—more valuable, in many ways, than the formal degrees hanging on their walls.

The choice is yours

So here we are. You've been given two paths:

1. Follow the conventional wisdom: make a plan, stick to the plan, keep your head down, and hope it all works out.
2. Develop a capacity for productive surprise: maintain your plan as a framework, but keep your antenna up for the unexpected opportunities, connections, and insights that often lead to your greatest achievements.

The first path is safer. It's more predictable. It's what most people will choose.

The second path is messier. It requires more discernment. It demands that you hold opposing ideas simultaneously—loving and hating institutions, planning and improvising, persisting and pivoting.

But that messier path is where the real magic happens.

The most successful people I know aren't just disciplined planners—they're also skilled improvisers. They don't just execute—they notice. They don't just persist—they adapt. They don't just compete—they learn from competitors.

And most importantly, they've developed the ability to surprise themselves. What about you?

EXERCISE: THE PRODUCTIVE SURPRISE INVENTORY

1. Write down three "HUH" moments you've experienced in the past month—things that caught your attention because they didn't fit your expectations or existing knowledge.
2. For each moment, ask yourself: What opportunity might be hidden here? What could I learn from this? What action might this prompt?
3. Identify one institution or system you've been viewing in oversimplified terms (all good or all bad). List three beneficial aspects and three problematic aspects of this institution.
4. Write down one competitor or rival you've dismissed rather than learned from. What specific qualities or strategies could you adapt from them?
5. List three unexpected sources of wisdom in your life—people, experiences, or resources that have taught you valuable lessons from surprising directions.

QUESTION TO REFLECT ON

When was the last time you were genuinely surprised by something that eventually led to growth or opportunity? What made you notice that surprise rather than dismiss it, and how might you cultivate more openness to such moments?

FIRST STEP

Choose one area of your life where you've been rigidly following a plan or holding a fixed belief. For the next week, approach it with intentional curiosity. Ask questions you haven't asked before. Notice details you've overlooked. Consider perspectives that contradict your assumptions. At the end of the week, reflect on what this experiment revealed that might influence your path forward.

FINAL NOTES FOR YOUR FINAL EXAM

Wow. I don't know what happened to you last year, but wow—a multi-ton truckload of stuff happened in my life (and I wrote this book, too). This has been an emotional rollercoaster for me. What I can tell you is this: trust your intuition.

I knew it was time for me to lead. I knew it was time for me to dedicate myself to my own work and to create a roadmap for people behind me. Turns out that launching and completing a project that I could create, mold, and bring to fruition was critical to my well-being and hopefully, yours.

What I went through reflects the journey I am asking you to embark upon.

Let me spend a few moments reflecting and providing a few final comments as you continue your personal and professional journey. First, I just want to thank you for getting to this point—the end of this book—and arriving at the launching point for a "new you" personally and professionally.

You might have guessed that I'm not a big fan of people that start stuff and don't finish the job. Any job you or I have ever done is both easier and harder when you're not alone. I really struggled with some of this content as I was pushed, pressed, and asked to scrap huge sections of thought leadership that I was passionate about, but it didn't fit what our collective team was trying to accomplish.

You are going to be faced hundreds of times in your life with the easy opportunity to quit. When you quit on the little stuff, you will quit on the big stuff.

When you quit on the big stuff, you become the guy that is bitter, resentful, and forgets the fundamental rule that occasionally, you need to look in the mirror.

In one reflective section I discussed a stream. During that time, I was going through a lot, and I could have just stopped writing this book and investing in the process. I decided to be the water going under, around, and over the impediments in the stream flowing down Peak 9. You can be the water, or you can be the sedentary rock—free will is beautiful or devastating—it's your choice.

The more successful you become, the more you will encounter scorpions, brambles, and beasts in your professional life. Envy and attack can be the part of the price of working hard and doing well for yourself. Remind yourself that the people attacking you aren't the people you want to continue climbing with. When you are doing the correct thing at the right time with the right intentions, you must shake off the people who are detractors.

When you aren't stuck in a rut, when you aren't afraid, and when you want to feel the sun on your face—the air gets thinner, the sun gets brighter, and you get sunburned. Even if you're not reckless, you can get injured—and for sure, your feelings get hurt. People who fear you, your power, and your courage will do some stupid things. Don't let them distract you or cause you to look away from your best interests. Be smart. Take care of yourself and those who genuinely are your friends.

Do not expect that it will get any easier as you succeed. It gets more complicated. More nuanced. The battles are bigger. The stakes are higher. So, don't just get older, get better. Your skin needs to get tougher, you need to listen more intentionally, and you need to speak less.

If you want some satisfaction, consider the average life of a scorpion is 3 to 8 years. When you contemplate your next 20-plus years, someone else will have stepped on your scorpion.

Here's the cheat sheet with the fundamental principles spelled out for you.

1. Change typically feels awful. Don't expect your evolution to be easy. It takes time, patience, and commitment. Don't accept participation trophies. Work to win and then hold the gold over your head.

2. Be irrational and set a couple of BHAG's: Big Hairy Audacious Goals. I've been stuck on 13-Ironman finishes and I just don't like the number. I know it's not rational, and it's not the number 13. But, at the end of the year, I will have crossed the finish line a 14th time. I won't be fast, I won't medal in my age group, I won't qualify for Kona. I'm ok with that. What

I'm not OK with is being stuck at 13. Set your BHAGs to get un-stuck and transform yourself into the unshakably confident rockstar that is just under the surface right now, within your grasp. Never let the fear of failure or inertia get you mentally and emotionally just pretending to try.

3. Risk offending someone by helping them. I wrote this book because I felt like I had an *obligation* to try to help with the lessons I have experienced over the past 30 years. Don't take any guff about how old you are or what your generation supposedly suffers from. My generation was too inwardly focused as I grew up- just like we accuse yours of being—and it took coaches, mentors, sherpas, and sounding boards to evolve me to where I am today. Be uncomfortably helpful. Take time to fix something for someone. Send a note that encourages someone who's hurting. You may wonder if you are wasting your most precious asset—your time. It's ok to wonder. Just act and help. You may not make a nickel. What you will be is a better human being making this world a better place to live and work in.

4. Finally, please do me a few favors:

   a. Seriously consider changing just one aspect of yourself and how you think, operate, and live from each part of this book.

   b. Write down what you are going to change, commit to these changes, and measure yourself on changes at regular intervals—like once a month. Some months you will move up the hill, some months you will fall back, and some months you will be stuck in neutral. That's how life works, so please tamp down your inevitable frustration.

   c. Buy this book as a gift for someone who really needs it or give them your copy, (just ask for it back as I assume you have highlighted and marked up your copy).

   d. Over the next few years, when life smacks you across the face, pick the book up again and re-read a section or two. Soup is always better the second day it is made, and you may feel the same about this book.

Just kidding about the final exam. Enjoy your personal journey and see you around my friend!

John

Juno Beach, Florida

or Breckenridge, Colorado—depending on the season

ACKNOWLEDGMENTS

As you've seen throughout the pages you've just read, I've had the help of many people in crafting this book. As I was writing it with your challenges in mind, I reached out to some extraordinary friends and colleagues whose experiences or perspectives I believed would motivate and enlighten you. My fervent hope is that, in each reflection you read from them, you were able to feel heartfelt encouragement, a strong hand pulling you up, and a force of nature pushing you ahead.

While you got their formal biographies at the end of their reflections, I now want to let you know how dear these folks are to me and why they generously shared their "learn from my mistakes as much as my success" stories so frankly.

Meet Remy Bernstein & Cooper Pickett: Digital marketing entrepreneurs who rose from ashes

I remember walking around the city in the financial district with Remy and Cooper as we went to a cramped, WeWork (remember that?) space where their team was cranking out content, developing websites, and going about a full range of advertising and communications work. Then COVID hit. Most people in their shoes would have done what most did: contract their staff and save themselves. Instead, Cooper and Remy pivoted with a pure focus on doing what was right—save peoples' jobs, take a pay cut, and figure it out so when times got better, they would still be all together. This is a tangible example of the young generation of entrepreneurs who refused to quit, expanded into new business lines, and grew despite odds that would crush most souls. In a world where employees quit every 15 months for a couple of grand more, Cooper and Remy engendered a sense of trust, loyalty, and transparency. They have this weird gene that I don't see very often; it's called "the Caring Gene." I hope you enjoy their story!

Meet Phil Buchanon: Cannon Financial leader and trusted advisor to professionals

Phil and I have known of each other since my Merrill Lynch days and worked together on projects for Ameriprise and Stifel. He and his firm, Cannon Financial, are recognized as industry thought leaders in wealth management, insurance, banking, and trust. When COVID struck, his firm was poised to capitalize on it because of their forward-thinking strategies—and capitalize they did, training hundreds of thousands of professionals. Phil created an amazing thought journal of his career for you to contemplate, regardless of what stage your career is in today.

Meet Chantalle Couba: Accomplished executive and organizational coach with real-life wisdom and academic gravitas

Chantalle and I became close when we went to the University of Pennsylvania together, earning our doctorates. She has always been better than me in everything—writing, communicating, patience, and the list goes on and on. As I am reminded by many, one of my advantages is that I'm a white man and with that comes privilege. Chantalle, along with others, had helped me see the need to give back and not only with a check. She has held some big jobs on Wall Street and now has a thriving consulting practice. The reason we get along so well is that she is a dude. I mean this in the most endearing and positive way I can, and if anyone is offended by this, I really don't care because I just made her smile!

Meet Ryan Hall: The biker who took the hard road and the high road to success

Ryan is married to my daughter Meggie. He is a wonderful human being, a highly educated and tatted up music bro who is both sensitive and caring (clearly due to his upbringing by his Mom). I have enjoyed watching his learning journey in the work world as well as his side projects like his long-form YouTube Channel depicting the travel that Meggie and Ryan do together all over the globe. His love for nature is unmatched and his ability as a vibrant, multi-faceted person to embrace the silence and stillness on a hike, in the snow, or wherever he ventures proves he is wise beyond his years. I'm blessed to consider him a third son.

Meet Jane Kim, M.D., EdD: Emergency room doctor and ever evolving human

Jane and I are lifelong learners, as our paths crossed at The University of Pennsylvania. I call her "Dr. Dr." because Jane is an ER physician and a Doctor of Education from Penn. She is clearly an underachiever!!! Not. Jane is also boss snowboarder and, oh by the way, runs an ER for the less privileged communities in New York. She is your typical Type A, hard charging, always winning leader who had an amazing epiphany. She shares some lessons to help you combat the stressors that can lead to mental, physical, and emotional breakdowns. She learned to say "no" and when to quit (for all the right reasons).

Meet Matt Livingstone: The athlete who doesn't know the words "slow down," "maybe not," or "it's too tough"

Matt has been my training partner, sherpa, and dear friend from the time we met at a bike shop when I was learning how to ride. We did a few Ironmans together until Gabby, his wife, weighed in against these long-distance tri's. So, he is now qualifying and doing even more ridiculous races like Mt. Blanc. While I can't hang with him on a run anymore, he is showing his elder respect by humoring me doing the Loop in Fairmount Park in Philly (there he will bang out another 20 miles after I collapse). In real life, Matt is a much lauded, extraordinary creative team leader with big bonafides in major branding and communications campaigns.

Meet Tony Sirianni: A brilliant entrepreneur who created the ultimate comeback after cratering

Tony and I had known of each other for years, but the meaning of our friendship crystalized when one of our mutual friends, Mike Mauer, died of COVID at age 50 at the start of the global pandemic. I had video chatted with Mike one day, and then the next day Tony called me to say Mike had died. I remember standing on a deck in Breckenridge looking at the absolute beauty of nature when Tony gave me the news. All I could think was that life can be cut short, so pay attention to what you're doing while you are here. Tony is what I would term a serial entrepreneur, and as you read his raw reflection, you would never imagine that in fact, everything he touches turns into gold.

Meet Brian Waelti: Financial Services Executive

Brian had the unenviable task of leading the on-boarding function for new "experienced advisor recruits" when we were both at Ameriprise. Leading biz dev is a thankless job when you are dealing with the finance people, leading on-boarding is a mercilessly thankless job when you must deal with the head of biz dev! Brian held some big jobs in financial services and the consulting world and shares the sacrifices and learnings you may have as you move jobs, geographies, and stretch assignments in your career.

Meet Phil Waxelbaum: A veteran chief executive who plays the long game to win

Phil and I have known each other from our Ameriprise days. Phil has held some big jobs on Wall Street and kept his humility and grace, despite the grandeur of being big man on campus. He has been a steadfast friend and business partner at all my stops as a trusted external search firm partner. He embodies integrity and honesty (something difficult to find in search.) What sets Phil apart is his humanness. When I was bought out by the private equity firm (don't feel sorry for me now!) my life crashed upon me because I felt I wasted four-plus years of my life building "The Team," only to see it destroyed. Phil was always there for me as I walked Juno Beach considering my next steps. Big learning from a great friend: we all have a next step.

Meet Nance Rosen: My ride-or-die in creating a book that would poke, prod, shock, inspire, and make you unshakably courageous

I'd like to conclude by spending a few moments sharing some thoughts about Nance Rosen, my editor. She helped me interpret my goals, thoughts, and experiences for this book and thus is an influence not just in my life, but now in yours as well. Often, great relationships start with an introduction by a common friend. This was the case for me as I discussed the concept of a new book with a friend, and she introduced me to Nance.

If you review Nance's bio, you'll see it's difficult to easily summarize who Nance is and the incredible value she delivers for clients, students, and friends. A line on her website (nancespeaks.com) says "My Job is Making You Succeed." With Nance, I have learned that this phrase is not hyperbole. Executive and Leadership Coach. Author. Professor. Confidant. Publisher. Visionary. Creator. Blogger. International Speaker. Corporate Trainer. Career Planner. (And, most recently survivor of the California wildfires and mudslides!) The descriptors and superlatives go on and on. While saying she's also got speed reading skills and a photographic memory helps, all these platitudes don't do Nance justice. I struggled writing this piece because Nance has been so incredibly valuable, insightful, and purposeful in the formation, evolution, and creation of this work.

Bottom Line? Brilliant person with a caring heart who gets stuff done.

How did the book come to fruition? After 30 years in financial services with a few firms, I wanted to turn my career into an investment that delivered a return to *you*—the generation coming up in corporate now. I wanted to give you the best, most realistic and relatable perspective about overcoming career hardships—and building confidence—even when really awful stuff happens. I also wanted to failure-proof you—to help you prepare yourself so you felt confident and in control no matter what happened.

When I committed to end my time in the corporate grind and challenged myself to write, I had a few pivotal ideas. I knew I wanted this book to make sense of my experience and distill what really mattered. It's fair to say that even when one person has a strong, original idea as I did, every good book has many contributors, large and small. Taking credit for intellectual capital is important. Celebrating people who help deliver it is more important, from my point of view.

At the beginning of our relationship, Nance and I basically interviewed each other. Did I want to create with her, and did she want to create with me? I probably came across a little gruff and maybe a "tiny" bit headstrong at the start as we decided yes, this will be a fun and transformational project that could help a lot of people.

Every project is a journey with twists and turns. What you read in this book is the result of many of those gyrations. Nance and I would meet once a week and just talk. I would send her content I thought was meaningful, and we would discuss it as she constantly questioned, probed, and listened—as every world class coach does. She would then have some "think-abouts" for me and some deliverables before the next week. Call it thought provoking homework to make me finally drop my hard, ingrained corporate shell. Every working meeting became almost a counseling session as she drew out a multitude of raw experiences that have been turned into teaching and learning moments, and homework for you. Occasionally, she would drop a comment or two about a connection we had from the past and I was like you know them? Or you read my stuff from when? Always prepared. Always doing her homework. Always pressing. Always probing. Always searching for better.

So together, we've gone through my life (and a few others) to help you live your best one.

Nance has become an awesome business partner. More importantly, she is a friend. I hope you've enjoyed OUR work!

ABOUT THE AUTHOR

As a well-regarded executive in the financial sector, John Pierce brings decades of real-life experience that serves as a model for the guidance and stories you find in *Unshakable Confidence*. Having navigated a career with companies of every size—from behemoths to those scaling up—and completed what soon will be 14 Ironman competitions, John's strategic outlook and bare-knuckle fighting spirit has given him a unique and powerful outlook that his consulting clients value.

Asked about himself and his approach to work and life, John shared these thoughts:

> I like putting out dumpster fires. I like fixing things. Just to clarify, I can't hammer a nail straight or do anything practical in a workshop or garage. But, after thirty years in the financial sector, I recognized that I am good at taking big rock problems, boiling the concepts down into digestible forms, explaining them in simple and understandable ways, and finally chunking out solutions that create solid foundations for companies to thrive long-term.
>
> Currently, I work with a select number of companies to help them overcome challenges that are often complex and stubborn—where conventional solutions and the current team have not made meaningful progress. That's my sweet spot.

When I was asked to reflect on my life and career so far, I realized nothing I've accomplished could have been predicted.

I grew up in the mid-west: Toledo, Ohio. "Mid-west" nice is real. During summers, we would leave the house in the morning and ride our bikes to a park and play, returning home for lunch when one of the Mom's rang a lunch bell. Then, back outside until we had to be home (when the streetlights went on).

I always had a job, even as a kid. Toledo has four seasons so during summer I mowed grass and delivered the Toledo Blade. When winter hit and snow came, I took my red shovel and worked shoveling driveways and sidewalks, and came home exhausted, with cash falling out of my pockets. That's when I found I like the concept of money. That never left me. I didn't have the "killer instinct" yet but I realized this cash thing was not bad.

I went to grade school at Our Lady of Perpetual Help and was not a good student, in fact, I was placed with the "slow kids." Now, I'm a Mensa Life Member. What I realized is that I was just a disinterested and non-motivated kid. High school in Toledo was at the best college prep school in the area, St. Francis De Sales. I started to emerge as the real me at SFS, but still no killer instinct and not an athlete. I ran the mile in track and was slow as can be—I didn't know back then I would never be fast, but I could go forever. It's that ability that account for how I have completed 13 full distance Ironman's (2.4-mile swim, 112-mile bike and a little marathon to finish the day). SFS challenged me although Brother Roth was kind enough to pass me in Spanish despite my complete incapacity for a second language. I still scratch my head wondering how my three kids have mastered Spanish, Russian, and German.

Later in life I gave back by being on the SFS Endowment Board for 20-years (well past the "maximum" of the established five-year term). Father O. finally let me off the hook.

SFS was where I started to develop a passion for things like black and white photography, girls, the fun of learning and developing life-long relationships. College was at The University of Cincinnati where I muddled through academically and grew up away from home. My Mom still will not forgive me when I drove my blue Buick Skyhawk away to college, paid for with snow shoveling cash, and left Toledo for good.

Post college, I didn't want to work for the firms that everyone seemed eager to join—like Proctor & Gamble or Cintas. Instead, I naively started a childcare company. It grew into five centers in three states, with 120 employees. Run by a clueless kid just out of college. It was a harrowing and energizing experience that showed I was more naturally an entrepreneur rather than a corporate guy. I wound up ignoring that for the next 30 years, when I sold my company and joined a succession of corporate employers, including Merrill Lynch, Ameriprise, Stifel, and Cetera. Being on my own left its mark, and I brought the entrepreneurial experience and swagger to each corporate role, mostly with success.

While I was trying to keep the childcare company afloat, I needed a stress outlet, so I started studying Tae Kwon Do with Master Ahn in Cincinnati. I learned a lot about myself as I earned my black belt. Forms (those routine moves that are essential practice elements)—Bad. Sparring and fighting (reacting in the moment)—Good. Fast forward to today, I remain better on my feet, on the fly, and dealing with challenges and problems using my intellect rather than creating PowerPoints or memorizing speeches. Now, I do a keynote speech once a quarter for firms where I know my message and style will have impact.

So, even today, Memorize—Bad. Dealing with complex problems and issues that scare others—Good.

In my first corporate job at Merrill Lynch, I started in Cincinnati and then had my world flipped on its head when this Ohio kid was sent to Philly. Amazing learning experience where I saw the real-life consequences when mentors can help or harm and where coaches can show you how to soar to the sun and teach you, if you are willing, to not let the wax feathers melt in the heat.

Merrill acquired an asset manager when I was running Philly, and I was sent to London a few times to learn how to deliver their capabilities to other field leaders. That's also where I earned my MBA from the University of London in International Finance, with my work focusing on the evolution of fee-based business.

I am an advocate of life-long learning, regardless of how you go about education. If you are not learning, you are stagnant. As I see it, if you are stagnant, you are dead.

After 14 glorious years at what was "Mother Merrill" where I did the obligatory stint in New York City, I went to Ameriprise. There I encountered 110 branch managers who had mostly recruited college kids just starting their careers. These managers had never recruited experienced advisors, which was my mandate.

I took on the brutality of cutting low activity-low performance managers and feeding the rock stars who delivered high performance-high activity. I also helped make transformational changes in careers and lives, by helping high activity-low effectiveness people reach the top ten percent of leaders.

I get so much intrinsic joy helping my clients become a one percenter because it does not just help them, it changes generations in that family. Getting the phone call that "you changed my life" is better than the money falling from my snow pants shoveling in Toledo. Pivoting a 120 plus year firm was a phenomenal, and at times, brutally difficult exercise and I was blessed to experience it and learn from it.

Before my last corporate role, I earned a doctorate from the School of Education at the University of Pennsylvania, in part because it was recommended by my coach. This achievement reflects my commitment to continuous learning and sheer will to finish what I start. Had I known how difficult producing my dissertation would be from start to finish, I may have never started. Sometimes naiveté is the gateway to something great. The result of that work provided some of the learning and seeds that make up this book.

My last role in corporate was in financial services, but away from employee firms to an independent broker dealer owned by a private equity firm. This was another situation where the CEO, during our interview, told me I had two options: incremental change or burn it down. He then said private equity is not patient (and I learned that the hard way), so I burned it down, and built the most effective high performing recruiting team, pound for pound, in the industry. After a liquidity event I had to sit out a year, and decided to use the time wisely—hence, *Unshakable Confidence* took shape along with my preparation for a 14ᵗʰ Ironman.

To re-cap: I work hard and like money; I wasn't dumb just not motivated; life-long learning is evidenced by my undergraduate, MBA, and Doctorate; I am slow as molasses but can go forever as evidenced by 13 Ironman finishes so far; I'm not great at following order (forms) and I like to fight (Black Belt), and help others win.

I've enjoyed amazing experiences at Merrill, Ameriprise, Stifel, and Cetera but the corporate grind is over for me. I'm focused on a limited number of corporate consulting clients, a few C-Suite coaching clients, and four keynotes a year.

I'd be remiss if I didn't tell you that while I have the courage to take on change and challenges, and am willing to try new things, fear is something I have learned to manage. To ground myself I have active practices that keep me steady: reading, yoga, journaling, exercise, and a faith practice. It's been fun writing this. While I was a little afraid that sharing my life's journey would seem like boasting, I realized that writing this is simply my truth. It is my life.

I suggest you take on your journey in the same way—with both courage and sensitivity to how you keep yourself emotionally, intellectually, physically, financially, and spiritually well. After you read the book, purchase another copy for someone you want to help, and implement your game plan!

JRP

www.ingramcontent.com/pod-product-compliance
Lightning Source LLC
Chambersburg PA
CBHW071327210326
41597CB00015B/1376